CONVERSE® ALL STAR™
FOOTBALL
HOW TO PLAY LIKE A PRO

A MOUNTAIN LION BOOK

John Wiley & Sons, Inc.
New York • Chichester • Brisbane • Toronto • Singapore

Copyright © 1996 by Mountain Lion, Inc.
Published by John Wiley & Sons, Inc.

The publisher and the author have made every reasonable effort to insure that the activities in the book are safe when conducted as instructed but assume no responsibility for any damage caused or sustained while performing the activities in this book. Parents, guardians, and/or coaches should supervise young readers who undertake the activities in this book.

Library of Congress Cataloging-in-Publication Data:

Converse all star football : how to play like a pro.
          p.   cm. — (Converse all star sports series)
      Includes index.
      Summary: Provides detailed instructions on how to play to the game, with tips from football stars Jeff Blake, Drew Bledsoe, and Kerry Collins.
      ISBN 0-471-15978-6 (pbk. : alk. paper)
      1. Football—Juvenile literature.   2. Football—Training—Juvenile literature.   [1. Football.]   I. Converse (Firm)   II. Series.
      GV950.7.C65   1996
      796.323—dc20   96-20833

Printed in the United States of America
10 9 8 7 6 5 4 3 2 1

CONTENTS

Introduction _____ iv

1 This Game Called Football _____ 1

2 The Quarterback _____ 11

3 Running Backs _____ 31

4 The Receivers _____ 41

5 Offensive Linemen _____ 53

6 Defense _____ 59

7 The Kicking Game _____ 73

8 The Game Plan _____ 81

Glossary _____ 89

Index _____ 91

INTRODUCTION

Football is one of the most popular and exciting sports in America. The game was first played in the eastern part of the United States around 1850. It was a lot like soccer, and points were scored by kicking a round ball over the goal line. Each team had thirty or more players on the field at once. Fans sat in their wagons or on fences. Players took off their coats, rolled up their sleeves, and played. As the game became more popular, eastern colleges started their own teams and made up more rules.

By 1900, teams were still kicking the ball, but they were running with it, too. On running plays, blocking and tackling became important, and football games became more like fighting than a sports contest. Several college presidents stopped football at their schools, and many people wanted to outlaw the game.

President Theodore Roosevelt, who was a football fan, called a meeting of college coaches to see what could be done to make football safer. At the meeting, several rules were changed, and suggestions were made for improving the protective equipment worn by the players. Football became a "gentleman's game," with the athletes playing all-out to win in the spirit of fair play.

Passing the ball didn't become popular until 1913 in a game between Army and Notre Dame. The Notre Dame quarterback threw several passes, and Notre Dame won the game.

Today, the ball is carried and passed more than it is kicked. There's youth league football, high school football, college football, and pro football. But some great football games are played in backyards and on playgrounds, right in your neighborhood.

One of the best ways to learn how to play football is to be on a team, but you can learn a lot from reading this book and playing with your friends. Chapter one tells you what you need to know about the basics of the game. Other chapters tell you about the job of each player on the team and give you tips for playing that position.

You'll want to read this book on your own, then share it with your friends. They'll want to play like pros, too!

To make the instructions as interesting as possible, we have included bits of information and trivia concerning various players, coaches and teams in the history of football. Their inclusion is not an indication of an endorsement of any product, but to enhance your enjoyment and learning experience.

CHAPTER 1

This Game Called Football

Football is one of the most exciting games to watch because there's so much action: the linemen slamming into each other, the quarterback firing off a long pass, the receiver running all out to catch the ball, the defensive end bringing down the receiver. There are fake plays, fancy footwork, and field goals.

What's even more exciting than watching football? *Playing* football, of course!

Football players are *athletes*—they run, they jump, they throw, they catch, they block, they tackle, they use their whole bodies to defeat their opponents.

So if you're a football player, then you're an athlete. But you're more than just an athlete, you're part of a *team*. A football game is a contest between two teams—us against them.

The Spirit of the Game

Being a good team member means staying in the *spirit of the game*. Staying in the spirit means that you play to help your team win, not to get the glory for yourself.

What Are We Fighting For?

In a football game, two teams of eleven players try to score points by kicking or running the football across their opponent's goal line. The team that has the most points when the game is over, wins.

Getting Started

Before you can play football, you need to know a little about the game.

The Football

The *football* is an oval ball, pointed on both ends and made of leather with a grainy texture. The football has laces on one side and a white band near each pointy end.

The Playing Field

Football is played outdoors on a rectangular field that is 120 yards long and 53⅓ yards wide.

The field is divided up by parallel lines, 5 yards apart. The lines at each end of the field are called *end lines*. Ten yards inside each end line is the *goal line*. The area between the goal line and the end line is the *end zone*. The lines on each side of the field are called *side lines*.

The *fifty-yard line* is the name given to the line across the middle of the field. The lines parallel to the fifty yard-line are named for the distances they represent from the goal. For example, the thirty-yard line is thirty yards from the goal (and twenty yards from the fifty-yard line).

Territories

The fifty-yard line does more than just divide the field in half. It divides the field into two *territories*. Each team guards their own territory (half of the field) from the other team. In order for a team to score points, they must move the ball to their goal line, which is at the far end of the other team's territory.

The Goal Posts

There are two goal posts, one in each end zone. The goal posts are shaped like a big H. The crossbar of the goal post must be 10 feet above the ground.

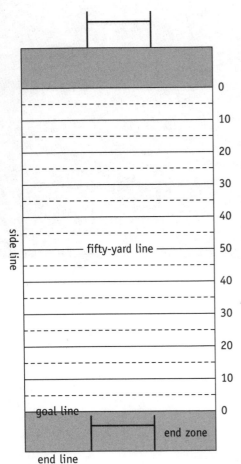

Equipment

Since football is a rough and tumble game, each player wears gear that helps protect him from injury. Equipment includes:

- a helmet made of unbreakable plastic that has a face mask and a chin strap.
- a mouth guard (teeth protector).
- pads to protect the shoulders, ribs, hips, thighs, and knees.
- pants, stockings, and lightweight shoes with cleats.
- a jersey (shirt) that's the color of the team. Each player is assigned a number which is printed on the front and back of his jersey.

The Players

Each team has eleven players on the field at one time. However a football team has many more than just eleven players. In fact, a football team is really made up of smaller teams: the offense, the defense, and the special teams.

The Offense

The job of the *offense* is to move the ball down the field, through the other team's territory, and across the goal line to score points. When your team has the ball in their possession, then your offense is playing on the field.

The Defense

The job of the *defense* is to stop the other team's offense from moving the ball toward their goal. When the other team has the ball, then your defense will be on the field, defending your territory.

Special Teams

In addition to the offense and the defense, a football team also has other, *special teams*. These special teams are used for kickoffs and punt returns (kicking plays).

Outside the Lines

WHO SAYS FOOTBALL IS AN ELEVEN-MAN GAME? The record for the longest run in NFL history is 99 yards. It was set by the Dallas Cowboys' Tony Dorsett against the Minnesota Vikings on January 3, 1983.

Incredibly, the Cowboys had only ten offensive players on the field when Dorsett made his run!

Playing the Game

Timing

The game is divided into four time periods (quarters), with a fifteen minute break after the first half.

The Kickoff

The ball is put into play at the start of each half with a *kickoff*. Before the game begins, the referee tosses a coin to determine which team will kick off first. The team that does not kick off at the beginning of the game will kick off to start the second half.

The ball is placed on a special tee (ball holder) at the forty-yard line in the kicking team's territory. The kicker runs toward the ball and kicks it as far as he can into the other team's territory (their half of the field). The receiving team catches the ball and runs it back up the field as far as they can before they are stopped by the other team.

The Line of Scrimmage

After the kickoff, and after the receiving team has moved the ball as far as they can toward their goal, the spot where the ball is resting is called the *line of scrimmage*. The line of scrimmage is an imaginary line that passes through the end of the ball and extends across the field from sideline to sideline. There are really two lines of scrimmage, one through each end of the ball. The small space (length of the ball) between the two lines of scrimmage is called the neutral zone.

Setting up to Play

One team's offense faces the other team's defense across the lines of scrimmage.

The Defense

The *ends* and the tackles stop the running backs when they are carrying the ball and try to tackle (sack) the quarterback before he can throw a pass. The *line backers* are supposed to tackle the running back with the ball and knock down or intercept short passes. The primary responsibility of the *corner backs* and *safeties* is to guard against passes. Corner backs guard against the faster, quicker receivers while the safeties usually try to prevent passes from being caught and protect against a run in case a running back gets beyond the line of scrimmage and the linebackers. Sometimes, a line backer, cornerback or safety will charge through the line (blitz) and try to sack the quarterback.

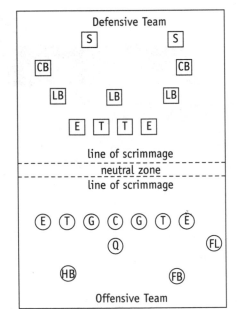

The Offense

The ends block the defensive linemen or linebackers and sometimes catch passes. The *tackles*, *guards* and *center* block for the quarterback and for the running backs. The center snaps the ball to the quarterback to start the play. The *quarterback* calls the plays, receives the ball from the center and hands off to the running backs, passes to the receivers or runs the ball himself. The *halfback* and *fullback* take hand offs from the quarterback and run with the ball, catch passes thrown by the quarterback or block for the quarterback and other running back. The *flanker* catches passes, blocks down field if he isn't catching the ball and occasionally runs with the ball.

Downs

When your team has the ball, you get four plays (tries) in which to move the ball forward 10 yards from the line of scrimmage. When your team sets up for their first play, we say that it is *first down and ten*, meaning that it's your first try and you have to move the ball ten yards.

Suppose you move the ball six yards forward on the first down. Then we say that it is *second down and four,* meaning that it's your second try, and you have four yards left to move the ball.

Your offense gets to keep trying until they either gain the whole ten yards, score a touchdown or field goal, or use up all four downs. If you gain the whole ten yards from where you started, you've made another first down, meaning that you get another four tries to get another ten yards. If you use up all four downs before gaining the ten yards, then the other team gets the ball.

Moving The Ball

There are three kinds of plays your team can use to move the ball toward the goal line:

Running Plays

In a running play, one of your offensive players runs the ball down the field.

YOU'RE NEVER TOO YOUNG

Chris Spielman, the Detroit Lions Pro Bowl linebacker who was also an All-America player at Ohio State, got his start early—when he was just five years old, he tackled his grandmother. When asked why he tackled her, Spielman said, "She walked through the door. She went to give me a hug and I took her out. I knocked her down, but she bounced back up. You could tell she was a Spielman." (You probably shouldn't try this on your grandmother!)

Passing Plays

In a passing play, your team's quarterback will pass (throw) the ball forward to a receiver, who catches it and tries to run it even farther down the field.

Kicking Plays

Your team's kicker punts (kicks) the ball up the field, or tries for a field goal.

Scoring

There are four ways to score in a football game: touchdowns, extra points, field goals, and the safety.

Touchdowns

When a player carries the ball across the goal line into the other team's end zone or catches a pass in the end zone, then he scores a touchdown for six points.

Extra Points

After a touchdown, the scoring team is allowed to try for extra points. The ball is set two yards back from the goal line. If the ball is run or passed into the end zone by the offense, it's worth two extra points. If the ball is kicked over the end zone and through the goal posts by the offense, it's worth one extra point.

Field Goals

A field goal is when a player kicks the ball through the uprights of the goal post. It is worth three points.

Safety

When a team has the ball in its own end zone and either loses the ball to the other team, or is stopped by the other team in the end zone, then the other team gets two points.

The Rules

There are many, many rules in football. You will learn most of them from your coach and you will learn some of them just by playing the game. Here are some of the primary rules.

You're not allowed to:

- tackle or hold anyone who's not carrying the ball. (However you can block players who don't have the ball.)
- try to hurt an opponent on purpose.
- trip, kick, or punch an opponent.
- move across the line of scrimmage before the ball is put into play by the center.
- "pile on" (jump on top of another player after he is already down).
- grab an opponent's face mask.
- have more than eleven players from your team on the field at any time.

The Officials

These are the referees in the striped shirts. They're out there on the field during the game, making sure that the rules are followed. If a rule is broken, then a referee will give that team a penalty (punishment), usually a loss of yardage. The referees blow a whistle to end every play.

The Coach

The coach is really a teacher. His job is to teach his players how to play the game and show them how they can become better athletes. The coach plans the strategy for each game and calls most of the plays.

Getting in Shape for Football

Athletes need to be in good physical shape in order to have the strength and physical skills to do their jobs. Staying in good shape also helps protect you against getting hurt.

Before playing football (or any other sport) you should always warm up your muscles by stretching them.

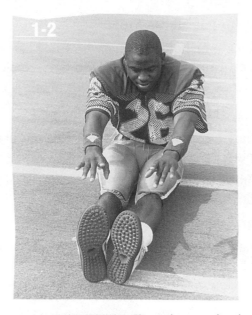

1-1 STRETCHING EXERCISES/HAMSTRING: Stretching is required at every level of competition. It is the best way to prepare for the severe physical stress that muscles will undergo during practice and a game. It will help prevent injuries. When doing the hamstring stretch, stand straight-legged, bend at the waist, and slowly reach for your shoe tops.

1-2 FRONT STRETCH: Sit on the ground and slowly lean forward as far as possible without bending your legs.

1-3 GROIN STRETCH: Sit with the bottoms of your feet together and pulled into your body as far as possible. Place the elbows inside the thighs just above the knee. Push outward and downward with the elbows.

1-4 QUADRICEP STRETCH: Lie first on one side, and then the other. Grasp the foot of the top leg foot and slowly pull it back.

1-5 HURDLER'S STRETCH: Sit and place one leg in front with the foot and toe pointed up. Pull the other leg to the side, fold the leg and foot backward until you feel a slight tugging along the front of the leg. Then lean forward over the straight leg and reach slowly for the toe.

Here are some stretches you can do before you practice or play in a game to help prevent injuries:

- Stand with your feet together. Keeping your knees straight, bend over and try to touch the ground in front of your feet with your finger tips. Only stretch as far as feels comfortable, and don't bounce or bob.

- While sitting, with legs outstretched in front of you, try to touch your toes.

- Sit and draw your feet up as close into you your body as possible without straining your muscles.

- Lie on one side, grasp your toe on the upper leg and pull it back toward your rear. Hold the stretch for fifteen seconds, roll over and repeat for the other leg.

- While sitting, place one leg out in front and bend the other leg behind you as if you were jumping over a hurdle. Lean as far forward as possible, tying to touch your knee with your forehead. Repeat for the other leg.

    Repeat all stretches five or six times. (Figures 1-1 to 1-5.)

Regular exercise (three or four times a week) will help keep you in shape and ready to play the game.

Exercises that you can do on your own to stay in shape include: jogging, sprinting (running fast for a short distance), and running sideways and backward.

Young players under the age of fourteen probably shouldn't lift weights or use weight machines. When you do work with weights, it's important to have an expert teach you the correct way to lift.

Make It Up, Play It Out

You and your friends don't have to be on a team to play football. Getting together for a game of *touch football* can be lots of fun.

Touch Football

You need ten or more players, a football, and a field with two goal lines. Divide your friends into two teams. One team defends one half of the field, and the other team defends the other half. Each team tries to move the ball over their goal line by passing or running it forward. Each team gets four downs (tries) for a touchdown, which counts six points. If you don't make a touchdown in four tries, it's the other team's turn.

Tackling is not allowed in touch football. The players only need to touch the ball carrier and he has to stop, but you need to touch him with *both* hands.

2

The Quarterback

The quarterback is the star of the team. His leadership and athletic ability can make a good team great or help an average team win. Troy Aikman, Brett Favre, Drew Bledsoe, Dan Marino, and Jim Kelly are famous quarterbacks because they can produce victories and championships. The quarterback's job is glamorous, but it is also very hard. If the team wins, the quarterback gets the credit, but if the team loses, he gets the blame.

The quarterback calls the plays for the offense. He spends many hours studying his team's game plan before he even steps on the field. He has to be ready to handle any defense the opponent might use, and he has to know what play will work best. On the field, the quarterback sets an example for his teammates, and he stays in the "spirit of the game," realizing that all team members work together to help their team win.

Calling the Play

As quarterback, your first job on the field is to *call the play* in the huddle (when your team gets together on the field just before the play).

When you call the play, look directly into the faces of your teammates and speak slowly and clearly, just loud enough for those in the huddle to hear. Then repeat the call to make sure everyone has heard it. Finally, say "Break!" to send the team to the line of scrimmage.

Checking the Defense

At the line of scrimmage, you already have an edge over the defense. You know when the ball will be snapped and what you want to do with it. Still, you need to know how the defense is set up. Look over the defense to see where their players are set up (be careful not to stare at the area where you want the pass or run to go). What should you do if you see that the defense is set up to stop the play you called?

Changing the Play

Many quarterbacks use a system of *audible* (spoken out loud) *play changes* to change the play at the line of scrimmage. Audible play changes are a secret code of words (for example, colors) and numbers that tell your team the play is being changed and what type of play will be run instead. For example, to change from a pass to a run, the code word might be "green." To change from a run to a pass, the code word might be "red." Each play will have a number. If you have a running play called "twenty-six" that you want to use instead of the pass play you called in the huddle, shout "Green twenty-six! Green twenty-six!" If you want to change from a run to a pass, shout "Red fifty-eight! Red fifty-eight!"

You should shout out the name of a color and a number before every play so the defense won't know if there is a change. For example, if you call a running play in the huddle and want to stay with that call, you might yell "Blue ninety-eight! Blue ninety-eight!—hut, hut, hut," and start the play. Neither the colors nor the numbers mean anything so the players ignore them, listening only for the snap count.

It's up to the players to listen closely to the quarterback's calls at the line of scrimmage. If anyone forgets the play, he should shout, "Check!" or even, "Tell me again," so the quarterback can repeat the play or re-form the huddle.

The Snap Count

The *snap count* is the number shouted by the quarterback that signals all the offensive players to action. You choose the number in the huddle and tell your teammates the name of the play and the snap count. For example, you might say, "Power run forty-six, *hut* (hike the ball) on three." When you line up behind the center, call out. "Hut one, hut two, hut three." On the sound of "three," the center snaps the ball to you and your teammates run the play.

Sometimes a player forgets the snap count. If he's a linemen, he can hold up, behind his back, the number of fingers of the snap count. If he's correct, you say "Right!" If he's wrong, you say, "No!" until he finds the right number. Running backs can ask you to whisper the snap count before taking their stance. If all else fails, all a teammate has to do is watch the ball until it has been snapped. If you forget the snap count—and this has happened to every quarterback—turn around and ask a running back to whisper it to you.

Outside the Lines

LOVE THAT NUMBER TWELVE AND NUMBER FOURTEEN
Four Pro Football Hall of Fame quarterbacks each wore the number twelve during their playing careers: Terry Bradshaw, Bob Griese, Joe Namath, and Roger Staubach. Three others wore the number fourteen: Dan Fouts, Otto Graham, and Y.A. Tittle.

Starting the Play

As quarterback, you need to know how to start the play.

The Stance
Stand behind the center with your feet about as wide apart as your shoulders. Keep your weight on both feet, but be ready to shift your weight to the foot that you will use to step away from the center after the snap. Lean forward and make sure that your hands are far enough under the center to receive the ball cleanly (Figures 2-1 and 2-3).

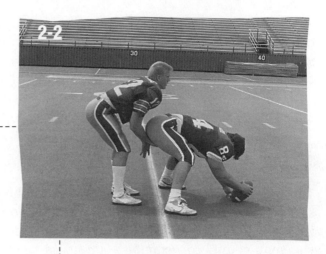

2-1 to 2-3 STANCE BEHIND THE CENTER: As the quarter-back, your first job is to check the defense and your own team's alignment. Then stand behind the center, feet shoulder width apart. Lean forward, place your hands under the center's butt where he snaps the ball.

Calling Signals

Call the signals loud enough for all players to hear. You may have to shout over the noise of the spectators.

There are two ways of calling signals:

1. The rhythmic count keeps an even tempo with the same pause between sounds: "Hut one...hut two...hut three." This type of count gets a team moving quickly and helps avoid mistakes.

2. The non-rhythmic count is used when the defense has caught on to the snap count. In the non-rhythmic count you might use longer pauses before each "hut," or you might use a quick series of "huts." You might even use a combination

of the two. For example, you might begin calling the rhythmic "hut-hut-hut," and then change to "hut". . . two-second pause . . . "hut-hut," or you might put the pause after the second "hut" (hut-hut" . . . two second pause . . . "hut") and so on.

The Snap

How you place your hands under the center depends on the type of *snap*.

There are two ways to snap the ball:

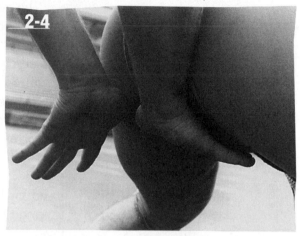

2-4 HANDS UNDER THE CENTER: How you hold your hands depends on whether you are left-handed or right-handed. Right-handed quarterbacks (shown) keep the right hand on top and the left hand slightly to the side

1. **A quarter turn** of the ball. The center gives the ball a *quarter turn* when handing it up. If you are right-handed, place the back of your right hand against the natural curve of the center's butt. Place your left hand, palm up, below your right hand, forming a V. (If you're a lefty, reverse your hands.) (Figure 2-4) As you set your hands, slap the center's butt where you want to receive the ball. Keep enough pressure so the center knows where the ball should go. When the snapped ball hits your hand, bring your bottom hand up to secure the ball. An advantage of the quarter turn is that it automatically places the laces of the ball across your fingers. You can throw or hand off the ball without feeling for the proper grip.

2. **A one-handed straight back with no rotation.** If the center does not rotate (turn) the ball, then the backs of both your hands should be on the center's butt with your thumbs touching each other. Slide your left thumb downward to form a natural groove for the ball.

Securing the Ball

Securing means making sure you have the ball under control (Figure 2-5). Fumbled (dropped) snaps are not the center's fault. If you don't get the ball with your top hand, or if it hits your bottom hand first, a fumble is likely. Keeping pressure on the center's butt will give him a solid target for placing the ball.

Once you have the ball, bring it back to your stomach, securing it with both hands so it won't get knocked loose before you can hand it off or drop back to pass.

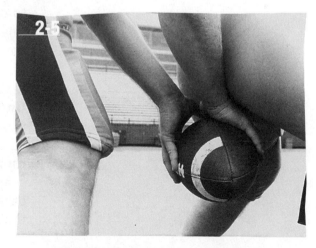

2-5 TAKING THE SNAP: As soon as the ball hits your top hand, your bottom hand should come up to secure it.

The Handoff

Make the *handoff* with your hands and your eyes. You must "see" the ball into the runner's hands. This means that you must watch the ball until it is in the runner's hands instead of just sticking it out there for him to grab. The runner will be looking for an opening at the line of scrimmage, not at the ball. He can take the ball only when he feels it touch his hands.

The running back will form a pocket to receive the handoff, either with his hands together or with his arms apart. If he is on the left side of you as he heads toward the line of scrimmage, his left elbow will be raised and his right arm will be underneath, forming the pocket where the quarterback must place the ball. If the runner is coming from your right side, the pocket is formed with his right elbow raised and his left arm underneath.

Either way, it's your responsibility to look at that pocket as you hand the ball to the running back.

Make sure you stand far enough away from the runner when handing him the ball so he has enough room to make his cuts (change direction). Extend your arm a bit, keeping it at belt level.

Types of Handoffs

There are the four types of handoffs to running backs:

1. **Front Out.** In the *front-out* handoff, you move to the right or the left, and hand the ball to the runner (Figure 2-6). Your first step after securing the ball from the center is in the direction of the play. If it's a dive play (meaning that the running back will be running straight forward into the middle of the defensive line), you simply turn around, go straight back and hand the ball off. If it's an off-tackle play (meaning that the runner looks for an opening next to one of his offensive tackles) from the I-formation (meaning that the runner is lined up directly behind you), you may first step backward to help the back see the line of scrimmage and find a good opening. Either way, your first step is in the direction the play is run.

2. **Underneath.** The *underneath* handoff starts off like a front-out handoff, but you cross the path of the running back before handing the ball to him. The back may start running to the right, then cut right or left as you take the snap and move backward. As you cross paths with the back, hand the ball forward while looking at the pocket that the back has formed with his hands and arms.

3. **Reverse Pivot.** The quarter-back moves right or left, then *pivots* on one foot with his back to the line of scrimmage and hands off the ball to a back coming from the other direction (Figures 2-7 to 2-9). If the play goes to the left, pivot on your left foot. If the play goes to the right, pivot on your right foot.

4. **The Toss.** *Toss* or pitch out plays are plays where the running back sweeps outside the defensive formation instead of running between defenders (Figures 2-10 and 2-11). You must bring the ball to your stomach on the snap, then pivot and pitch the ball to the back as he begins to run wide (to the outside). Deliver the ball in front of the runner, aimed at his chest or stomach, so he can continue running in full stride.

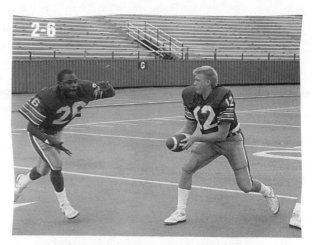

2-6 FRONT-OUT HANDOFF: After taking the snap, turn to the direction of the play, placing the ball into the natural pocket the running back has formed with his arms and side.

After any handoff, you should continue running as if you still have the ball. This follow-through will distract the defense.

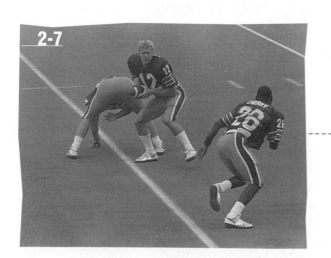

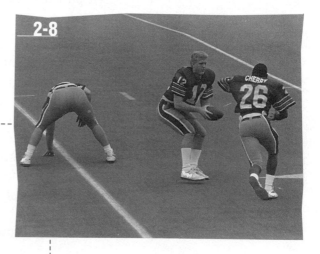

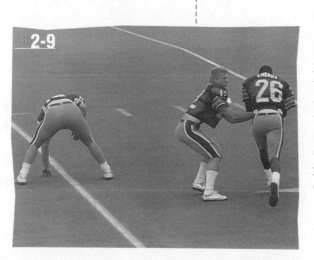

2-7 to 2-9 REVERSE PIVOT HAND-OFF: First pivot on the foot closest to the direction where you will eventually turn (right foot on a play to the right side and vice-versa). Face your body opposite to where you will hand the ball off and turn your back to the line of scrimmage. Your pivoting will take you to the handoff spot. You can then execute a faking motion by bringing your hands back into your stomach to confuse the defense.

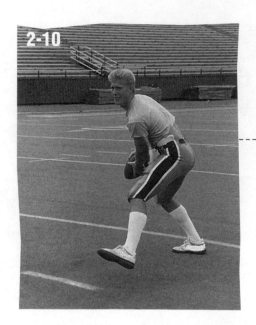

2-10 and 2-11 TOSS or PITCH OUT: Turn in the direction of the play, with your shoulders squared toward the running back. Toss the ball underhand using both hands. Aim for the central mid-section of the back.

Faking a Handoff

Faking a handoff can really fool the defense if it's done correctly. Secure the ball in both hands, place it near the runner's hands, then pull it back and hand it to another back.

The Draw Play

The *draw play* can fool the defense into thinking that you're going to throw a pass when it's really a running play. You must act like you're going to throw a pass as you move back for the handoff. This should get the linebackers and defensive backs moving backward, and they will be easier for your linemen to block. When running a draw play, don't "see" the ball into the runner's hands until you actually hand off the ball. Since you can't look for the runner as you move backward, he must position himself to get the ball while avoiding a collision. Timing is important and must be worked out in practice sessions.

Play Action

Play action is a pass play that looks at first like a running play. It can be successful when the team's running game is going well and the linebackers and defensive backs have begun to crowd the line of scrimmage.

You must fake handing off the ball before continuing back to throw the ball. The more realistic you fake the handoff, the better your play action will be. A lazy faker who goes through the motions with one hand or half-heartedly points the ball toward the runner while dropping back, fools no one. Give a good fake and keep the ball hidden after pulling it back until it is time to set up and throw.

The Passing Game

The quarterback has to be an expert passer. There is more to passing than standing in the pocket and throwing the ball. You need to pay attention to the details.

Starting

Your stance behind the center for a pass play is the same as for a running play, so the defense won't know if it's a pass play or a running play. As you get more experienced, you can cheat a bit by placing your getaway foot (left for righties, right for lefties) just slightly deeper than the other foot. Don't try this maneuver until you've mastered the basic stance.

When the ball is snapped, the laces should hit the fingers of your throwing hand. That way, you will be ready to throw before dropping back.

Once you have a firm grip on the ball, bring it in toward your stomach as you turn to drop back or move to your throwing area. With both hands, bring the ball to the front of your chest.

From the moment the ball is snapped, you have only three or four seconds to throw the ball, so get to the throwing area as fast as you can. The quicker you set up, the sooner you can see what's happening downfield.

Getting into Position

Here are two ways to get in position:

1. **Turn and Sprint Back.** *Turn* your non-throwing side away from the center of the field and *sprint* (run) to the "pocket." (In this case, the pocket means the area between three and seven yards from the center that's protected by the offensive linemen.) Set up to pass.

2. **Backpedal.** *Backpedal* (back up quickly) to the pocket. When backpedaling, you can see the entire defense and spot any blitzes that might be coming. (A blitz is when extra defensive backs rush (come at) the quarterback. Backpedaling is usually a shorter drop back than a turn and sprint back, and you will reach the throwing spot a second later.

Pass Drops

There are five *pass drops*. Two of them are passes straight back from the center to the pocket and the other two are sprint outs.

1. **Three-Step Pass Drop.** Take *three steps* backward, then step up and throw. You must set up fast and throw the ball before the defensive linemen can recover from blocks. The ball's path, is much straighter on the three-step drop than on the five- and seven-step drops.

2. **Five-Step Pass Drop.** (Figures 2-12 to 2-20) Sprint back *five steps* (six or seven yards). You are now ready to throw. Use the five-step drop for medium-range passes. Since there is little time to wind up and throw, your arm strength and throwing speed are very important.

3. **Seven-Step Pass Drop.** The *seven-step* drop takes you nine or ten yards behind the line of scrimmage. Your first four steps should be longer than normal. The last three are shorter to give you good balance. On the last step, bounce forward to the throwing position. This helps the offensive lineman form the pocket. There is room for you to step up and allow your blockers to force the pass rushers (defenders) to go beyond you, or you can stay put if the defender comes underneath (between you and the center)

4. **Sprint Out.** In the *full sprint-out pass* you can throw in the direction that favors your dominant arm (right for righties, left for lefties). Or you can throw "against your body," (in the direction opposite your throwing arm). Don't throw in front of the receiver. Throw directly to him because your momentum and his will bring the ball to an intersecting point. When throwing against your body, you will be most effective if, before releasing the ball, you "open" your hips (actually turn them toward the receiver) and set your throwing shoulder so that you face the receiver. The sprint out is most effective when the quarterback has run the ball on "keepers." (Keepers means that he is carrying the ball himself instead of handing it off.)

2-12 to 2-20 FIVE-STEP PASS DROP: Drop back as quickly as possible; look downfield as you sprint back to the pocket. Once you finish your steps, bounce back into the throwing position. Face the target and throw.

5. **Semi-Sprint.** In the semi-sprint, you move to the right (to the left for lefties), arrive at the set-up point, and throw immediately. The semi-sprint is useful in stopping the defense from aiming blitzes at one area.

Ready . . .
Aim . . . Throw!

You must grasp the ball firmly enough to guide it on the proper path. The bigger your throwing hand, the closer you can place it to the center of the ball.

The Grip

Have at least one finger on the laces. In a good *grip*, your thumb is underneath, your ring finger is on the seam, and your other three fingers are on the laces (Figures 2-21 and 2-22). Use your fingertips to control the ball so it won't rest in the palm of your hand and cause a sidearm throwing motion. Balls thrown with fingertip control produce pure overhand motion, proper follow-through, and a good spiral, keeping the ball in the air the least amount of time.

2-21 and 2-22 GRIPPING THE BALL: Spread your fingers as wide as possible and with as many fingers as possible on the laces. The thumb should rest stretched out. Place your thumb underneath toward the tip of the ball. Grasp the ball with the fingers and do not cradle it in your palm.

Throwing the Ball

Push the ball into the *throwing position* by raising it to ear level. If you hold the ball near your chest, you will have to lift it up to throw it, which costs time, and the receiver might be covered or the defenders might block your throw.

Move the leg opposite your throwing arm slightly upward and point your non-throwing arm toward your receiver. Turn your hips toward him. Start moving your arm forward with your wrist locked. Keep the foot opposite your throwing arm on the ground, so you are ready to shift your weight. Release the ball just past your head. To throw a ball low, release it a split second later

2-23 to 2-29
THROWING THE BALL:
Drop back to the pocket, bring your hands into your chest, feet shoulder width apart.

than for passes that need more height. Your wrist will snap as the ball is released, propelling the arm downward and bringing you into a squared-up position with the receiver. Remember to follow through (Figures 2-23 to 2-29).

On-the-Knee Drill

This drill is good for warming up before practice and for improving your throwing skills. Get down on your right knee (left for lefties) and place your left foot in front of you for balance. Hold the football in both hands in front of your chest. Look at your target or receiver as you bring the ball back and above your shoulder with your right hand (left for lefties). Continue looking at your target as you bring your throwing arm forward and release the ball (Figures 2-30 to 2-32). Practice throwing straight, and on angles to the right and left.

2-30 to 2-32 ON-THE-KNEE DRILL: Throwing full distance when the arm isn't loose is likely to cause injury. Here'a a drill to avoid injury, build arm strength and practice proper throwing mechanics in the upper body. Kneel on one knee, same side as your throwing arm. Toss a dozen balls at five-yard intervals starting at 10 yards and progressing to 30 yards. As you draw back your hand into the throwing position, shift your weight to your rear leg. Step toward your target and let your elbow of your throwing arm lead the way. Finish the throw by moving your hand and arm diagonally across your body so that your throwing hand completes its movements just below your opposite hip.

Types of Passes

Here are six types of passes that make use of wide receivers and tight ends:

1. **Outs.** The *quick square-out* is a five-yard pass thrown on a three-step drop. Throw the ball low, and in front of the receiver, forcing him to come back to catch the ball so the defender can't catch it. The *hitch* is similar to the square-out, except the receiver goes five yards, then turns and faces you without breaking toward the sideline. Quick outs and hitches are good first down passes.

2. **Slant.** The *slant* is thrown on a three-step drop to a receiver running through the defense on a forty-five degree angle. Throw the ball low, but do not force the receiver to reach or leap, exposing his back to a hard hit. This is a good pass to use in man-for-man coverage (where each defensive player is covering (staying with) one offensive player. It is not good in zone coverage (where each defender is covering an area of the field) because there is too much defensive traffic.

3. **Comeback Patterns.** In a *comeback* pattern a receiver runs fifteen or twenty yards down the sidelines and jams on the brakes to drive the defender backward. Before the defender can recover, the receiver runs back toward the ball. You must throw the ball before the receiver makes his comeback move. Throw low, so the receiver can protect the ball and go down without taking a hard hit in the back.

   In the *hook*, the receiver looks for an opening in the middle of the field between linebackers. When he finds the opening, he comes back toward you, and you throw the ball low to protect it from the defender.

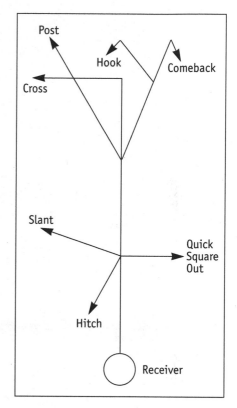

4. **Crossing Patterns.** *Crossing patterns* are thrown on a seven-step drop to a receiver who runs fifteen to twenty yards downfield and then cuts across the middle. When there is man-for-man coverage, lead the receiver away from the defender. If it is zone coverage, throw the ball as soon as the receiver makes his break. Throw it low, so the receiver isn't forced to extend his body. That way, you can save him from blind side hits.

5. **Post Pattern.** In the *post* pattern, the receiver starts downfield, then breaks toward the goal post. Throw the ball with a good arc and to the outside, so the receiver can run under it as he moves toward the sideline. Don't use this play when the defensive cornerbacks are playing deep (far from the line of scrimmage).

6. **Streak Pattern.** In the *streak* pattern, the receiver runs straight downfield.

Post and streak patterns are also known as "the bomb." Post and streak passes can be thrown from a seven-step drop. They can also be thrown quickly from a three-or four-step drop in blitz situations where receivers automatically adjust their routes to go deep because they have man-for-man coverages.

Swing and Screen Passes

These are two passes that specifically involve running backs:

1. **Swing Pass.** In the *swing* pass, a running back wheels out of the backfield on a rounded route toward the sideline, then heads downfield. You throw the ball out in front of him after he has straightened his route. This will make him increase his speed and generate the power to break tackles.

2. **Screen Pass.** For a good *screen* pass, you need patience, courage, and acting ability. For the regular, or *slow screen*, the offensive line and a back will brush block (block and then release) the pass rushers while you drop farther back in the pocket. The back runs to either side, where the offensive linemen form a blocking line. You continue looking downfield as if to pass. Take one last look to be sure there are no defenders in the middle of the screen before lofting the ball over the heads of the onrushing (coming toward you) defenders. If the play breaks down, throw the ball at the receiver's feet or take the sack (allow yourself to be tackled).

In the *read screen*, the quarterback first looks downfield, hoping to spot an open receiver and fool the defense into thinking that a long pass is coming. If the downfield receiver is covered, then pass to a back on the outside who has one or two blockers moving with him. In the *quick screen*, a wide receiver or tight end takes one or two steps downfield but quickly comes back to pick up a couple of blockers and receive the pass. Start with a play-action move to freeze the defense. Then throw the ball in front of that receiver to get him moving forward again.

Throw on the Run Drill

This drill will help you learn to throw on the run and to aim directly at a receiver. Two quarterbacks run along parallel lines about ten yards apart and throw the ball back and forth. Remember to turn your shoulders toward the receiver when you throw the ball.

Make It Up, Play It Out

Here are two fun games that will help you improve your passing.

Quarterback Toss

You need two or more players, a field, and ten or more targets. (You can use Frisbees, flags, jackets or whatever else you have on hand for the targets.)

Set the targets around the field and decide on which will be the first target. The players take turns throwing their footballs at the target. You get one point each time you hit the target. Then take turns throwing at the next target, and the next, and so on. After throwing at all the targets, the player with the most points wins the game.

Roll Ball

This is a game that you can play all by yourself. It will help you learn how to throw a pass to a moving receiver so that he can catch it without slowing down. You need your football and a soccer ball, volleyball, or basketball.

Pretend that the soccer ball is the receiver. Kick or roll the soccer ball down the field, then try to throw the football so that it lands on the soccer ball or right in front of it. See how many tries it takes for you to get ten hits.

Keep Focused

Five Basic Steps in Throwing the Ball

1. Get the proper grip.
2. Raise the ball to the side of your head.
3. Face the receiver.
4. Lead the way with your throwing elbow. Your wrist is locked and you release the ball just past your head.
5. Follow through into a squared-up position.

28

When did you first become interested in sports?

When I was about four years old. My dad played in the Canadian Football League.

Who was the biggest influence on your early sports life?

It was my dad because of his professional career and then working as a coach. I wanted to do what my father did.

What role did your dad play in your early sports career?

I have always appreciated that he inspired me to play, he didn't make me play. He always made it seem like fun.

Do you have any special advice for kids of how to approach playing sports?

Always do your best and don't ever give up.

Did you ever have any setbacks playing in the peewees?

We make mistakes in the NFL in every game. Making mistakes is part of the game, but you can never let them get you down.

You have played high school, college and pro football. What is your greatest triumph in sports?

Being able to prove myself as an NFL quarterback and then being selected to play in the 1996 Pro Bowl.

Running Backs

Running Backs do four things for the offensive team:

1. They block.

2. They take the ball (the handoff) from the quarterback, then "rush" (run it forward) to gain yardage.

3. They catch passes, then run to gain more yardage.

4. They fake (fool the other team).

Like the quarterback, the running backs are stars of the game. Running backs often make "big plays." A big play is any very important play that helps win the game. A big play can be a long run for lots of yardage, or catching a long pass near the goal line when time is running out and your team needs a touchdown in order to win.

Running backs are:

- **Fast.** They can dart through small openings and change direction in a flash.

- **Sure-Handed.** They can catch passes and they rarely fumble (drop the ball).

- **Powerful.** They are strong enough to block (stop) defenders and they can blast their way through the defense.

- **Fearless and Unselfish.** They are unafraid to block for another back or to take a hit (get tackled).

- **Disciplined.** They do not move before the ball is snapped.

- **Smart Runners.** They remember their plays and they can recognize what the defense is doing and change the plan if needed.

Getting the Ball

As a running back, you will get your assignment from the quarterback in the huddle. He will call the play, letting you know whether you will be carrying the ball, blocking, faking, or going out for a pass.

The running backs set up in the backfield (meaning they are behind the quarterback) so they will be ready to take a handoff or sprint (run) forward to catch a pass.

How you set yourself up depends on which *formation* your team will be using for the play. A formation is the way the players are arranged on the field. Two formations that are used often are the *pro set* and the *I-formation*.

Pro Set

In the *pro set*, the two running backs set up five to seven yards behind the quarterback, with one back out to the right of the quarterback, and the other back out to the left of the quarterback.

Sometimes, in this formation, the running backs are lined up straight behind the offensive tackles. Other times, each running back is lined up straight behind the space between a guard and the center (Figure 3-1).

The Stance

The stance used by the backs in the pro set formation is a *three-point stance*, meaning that you have three points of contact with the ground—your two feet and one hand.

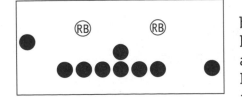

Place your feet a shoulder's width apart with one foot slightly back. Lean forward and place the fingertips of your dominant hand on the ground. Rest your other elbow against your leg, just above your knee. Keep your weight balanced evenly on both feet. Keep your back parallel to the ground. Keep your eyes straight ahead and don't look at the area that you will be running to. That might "tip off" (tell) the defense what your plan is.

I-formation

In the *I-formation*, two running backs are set up behind the quarterback with one back directly behind the other one (Figure 3-2). The back closest to the quarterback is known as the *fullback*. If you're the fullback, your toes should be five yards back from the front tip of the ball. The back that is the farthest from the quarterback is known as the *tailback*. If you're the tailback, your toes should be seven yards back from the front tip of the ball.

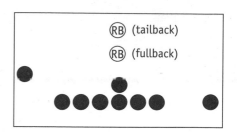

The Stance

In the I-formation, the two backs each use a different stance. If you're the fullback (closest to the quarterback) use the three-point stance, just like in the Pro Set.

If you're the tailback, use a *two-point stance*, meaning that you have two points of contact with the ground—your feet.

Place your feet a shoulder's width apart, keeping your feet parallel with each other. Lean forward slightly and rest your hands on your hips. You will be hunched over a little, but you can still see clearly over the top of the fullback.

3-1 PRO SET: Two running backs line up in three-point stance five yards behind the line of scrimmage. Remember to keep your eyes looking straight ahead.

3-2 I-FORMATION: Two running backs line up directly behind the center and quarterback, forming an I. The back closest to the quarterback is the fullback; the tailback is two yards behind the fullback.

This drill will help you get used to the proper stance, and give you practice coming off the line of scrimmage.

The running backs line up and take their stances. The coach looks over each player's stance and gives suggestions for improvement. The coach gives the running backs the play direction and snap count. On the correct count, the players explode out of their stances and sprint for ten yards. Then everyone turns around and repeats the drill in the other direction. Plays should be run both to the left and to the right.

The Handoff

The quarterback is responsible for *handing off* (giving) the ball to you. You are responsible for forming a "pocket" into which the quarterback will place the ball.

Make the pocket with your arms by placing one arm across your chest and the other across your body at your waist. The thumb of your upper hand should point downward and the palm should be turned slightly outward. Your bottom arm should lay against your jersey. Spread the fingers of your bottom hand so they will be ready to grasp the rear of the ball.

Never look for the ball. Your eyes should be focused on your path to the line of scrimmage. When you feel the quarterback place the ball into your pocket, grip the front nose (end) of the ball with your upper hand and the rear nose of the ball with your bottom hand. Secure the ball against your chest.

Avoid Fumbling

To avoid *fumbling* (dropping the ball), be sure that both your hands cover the ball until you've run at least five yards beyond the line of scrimmage. When you're in the clear, switch the ball to one arm, by placing the rear nose of the ball under your armpit, and cupping the front nose of the ball in your fingers. Cover the ball with your other hand to protect it even more.

Catching the Pitch Out

When catching a toss from the quarterback, as a running back must you must watch the ball all of the way into your hands. Make a target for the quarterback by holding your hands in front of your chest. You should catch it with your hands, not off of your pads. Make certain you have tucked the ball away securely before you make a move and head up field with the ball. (Figures 3-3 to 3-5.)

3-3 to 3-5 CATCHING THE PITCH OUT: Begin by stepping sidewards in the direction of the toss from the quarterback. Drag your trailing foot momentarily so that you make yourself an easy target for the quarterback. Don't forget to secure the ball as soon as you catch it.

Running with the Ball

Once you have the ball, your job is to run with it far enough to make a *first down*. When your offensive team goes out on the field to play, you get four plays (tries) in which to move the ball forward ten yards from where you started.

When your team sets up for the first play, we say that it is *first down and ten*, meaning that it's your first try and you have to move the ball ten yards.

Suppose you move the ball six yards on your first try. Then we say that it is *second down and four*, meaning that it's your second try, and you have four yards left to move the ball. You get to keep trying until you score, or gain the whole ten yards, or use up all four tries. (If you use up all four tries before you score of gain all ten yards, then the other team gets the ball.)

Once you gain the whole ten yards from where you started, you've made a first down, and you get four more tries to gain another ten yards from that spot.

When you're carrying the ball, you always need to know how far you have to run in order to make a first down, and you need to be determined to get there. You don't want your team to have to wait until your fourth (last) try to get a first down. You want to get a first down on every play!

Once you've run far enough to get the first down, you may find that you're in the clear and you can gain more yards, maybe even go all the way to the end zone for a touchdown!

Stumble Drill

This drill will teach you to keep your balance while running with the ball. It is also good practice for keeping the ball secure.

Line up on the goal line with a football in the carrying position. Run down the field, and at the next yard line, reach down with the hand you use to cover the ball and touch the yard line with your palm, which will cause you to stumble. To get your balance back while continuing to run, raise your head up, stick out your chest, and drive forward with your knees. As you get your balance back, shift the ball to the other arm and be ready to touch the next yard line with your other palm. Continue running down the field, switching hands and touching the yard lines, until you get to the twenty-five yard line. Then turn around and run back up the field, repeating the drill.

Run with Your Eyes, Too

Run with your eyes as well as with your feet and legs. This means that you must always be looking where you are going, and at the same time you must be aware of where the defenders are.

You will be looking to run through the "hole" (open area) that is supposed to be made by your blockers, as planned in the huddle. However, the hole may be in a different place because the defenders may have shifted position, or the defenders may have changed the direction of their charge. It's up to you to change your run in order to get to the hole.

Making Cuts

When running for the hole you should run in as straight a line as possible so that it will be easier for you to *make cuts* in any direction if needed. Making a cut means to change direction suddenly.

Beware of Stripping

Defensive players may try to "strip" the ball from you. Stripping means that the defender will force your arms apart causing you to drop the ball.

Sometimes you will be attacked by two defenders at once. The first defender will tackle you, hoping that the force of the tackle will knock the ball loose, then the second defender will go after the ball. To avoid being stripped of the ball, hold it very tightly against your chest and remember to cover it with your other hand. Lean over the ball slightly to protect it even more.

Faking

To be a good running back, you have to be a good actor. Part of your job is to *fake*, or fool the defenders into thinking you are carrying the ball when you're not. That will cause them to come after you instead of the real ball carrier, and that gives the real carrier a better chance at making the first down or even a touchdown.

A good fake starts with the quarterback. He must make the fake handoff look real. You finish the act by running with the fake ball. To make the defenders think you have the ball, grab your elbow with your other hand and pull the elbow down slightly. Hunch your shoulder over your "fake" ball and run. If you get tackled, it means you did a good job of fooling the defender. If you're not tackled, look for someone to block.

Blocking

As a running back, you will sometimes have to block (stop) a defender. There are four basic blocks used by running backs: the kick-out, the loco, the cat, and the bull.

1. **The Kick-Out.** Use the *kick-out* when you are blocking for another runner who will be going to the outside (around the end of the defensive line). Aim for the outside hip of the offensive tackle, then block the first defender who shows up on that side of the tackle. Make contact on the defender's inside number (number on his jersey), with your arms, lifting him up. Once you make contact, keep your feet moving in small, fast steps. Try to keep your body between the defender and the ball carrier.

2. **The Loco or Straight Ahead.** Use the *loco* when you're leading the runner *straight ahead*. Launch yourself at the defender, aiming to make contact just below his shoulder pads. As you make contact, keep your feet moving and keep driving the defender in the direction you want him to go.

3. **The Cut Block.** In this block, you want to *cut* off the defender before he has a chance to go after the quarterback. This block gives you the power to flatten defenders that are bigger than you are. Speed is the most important thing here. When you are two yards in front of the defender, pick up your speed. Keeping your head up and your back flat, dive at the shin of his outside leg. Your dive should feel like it would if you were diving into the shallow end of a swimming pool. If you're fast, he'll go down.

4. **The Bull Block.** The *bull block* is used when the quarterback is threatened before he can get off the pass.

Keep your elbows at your side, and your fists clenched. When the pass rusher (defender who is after the quarterback) gets within a yard of you, go after him. Don't wait for the pass rusher to make contact with you first. If you do, his forward motion will knock you down, or into the quarterback. You must explode forward, and attack with both forearms. Make contact no lower than his chest. If possible, move him to the outside, away from the quarterback.

Outside the Lines

RUNNERS BY THE NUMBERS

1. Walter Payton is the NFL's number one rushing leader, with 16,728 yards.

2. O. J. Simpson and Earl Campbell gained 200 or more yards in two consecutive games.

3. Herschel Walker gained 1,500 or more rushing yards in three consecutive seasons at Georgia.

4. Earl Campbell holds the NFL record for the most games, four, in a season gaining 200 or more rushing yards.

5. Barry Sanders' NCAA record at Oklahoma State is for rushing 200 yards in five consecutive games.

6. Ernie Nevers holds the record for rushing six touchdowns in one game (November 28, 1929)—the NFL's oldest standing record.

7. Eric Dickerson gained 1,000 or more yards in seven consecutive games.

8. Jim Brown earned eight NFL rushing titles during his Cleveland Browns career

Playing by the Rules

You are allowed to help the runner or the passer by blocking for him, but you are not allowed to:

- Help the runner by pushing or lifting him.

- Grab or tackle an opponent with your hands or arms.

- Kick or knee an opponent.

- Trip an opponent.

- Hit an opponent's face, head, or neck with your hand, forearm or elbow.

- Grab an opponent's face mask.

- Block or tackle anyone after the ball is dead.

The Passing Game

Good backs must be able to catch a pass, secure it against their body, and run with it.

Before you run your *pattern* (the route assigned to you by the quarterback in the huddle), look over the defense. If you see an extra linebacker move toward the line of scrimmage, the defense may be running a "blitz." A blitz is when one or more extra players rush (come at) the quarterback to tackle him. When you see a blitz coming, you must give up your plan and block the blitzer.

Pass Patterns

A *pass pattern* is a plan for how far the running back will run, where he'll turn, and at what point he will catch the ball.

There are three types of pass patterns:

Patterns from behind the Line of Scrimmage

These are passes that are thrown and caught *behind the line of scrimmage*. They are short and quick.

Close-in Patterns

Close-in passes are caught within ten yards beyond the line of scrimmage.

Deep Patterns

When the quarterback throws *deep*, he is throwing the football downfield, usually fifteen to thirty yards or more. These are the long passes.

Make It Up, Play It Out

Here's a game for three players that will sharpen your pass pattern skills.

Pass Pattern

All you need to play this game is a field, a football, and three people. There are two teams: one is made up of the quarterback and receiver, and the other team is the lone defender. The quarterback and receiver huddle up and decide what pass pattern to run. Then they run it and the defender tries to intercept the pass. If the pass is complete, the quarterback and receiver get one point. If the defender intercepts the ball, he gets two points. The first team to get twenty-one points wins the game.

A Checklist for Running Backs

1. Check the defense before settling into your stance by looking left and right, then keep your head and eyes straight ahead.
2. Start with the correct stance for the play.
3. Go into motion on the snap, and sprint at top speed.
4. Don't look for the ball on handoffs. You'll feel the ball when the quarterback puts it in your pocket.
5. Keep the ball covered by both hands until you're in the clear.
6. Keep your head up and use your side vision when running to keep track of what's happening around you.
7. Hold the ball tight to your body at all times to avoid fumbles.
8. Always know how far you have to run to get the first down.

The Receivers

P ass receivers are the offensive players that carry
the ball and make the touchdowns. Receivers are known for
their leaping, diving, and soaring catches, for their ability to
turn simple catches into big gains, and for their speed and
agility. Jerry Rice, Anthony Carter, Andre Reed, Art Monk,
and Michael Irvin are some famous NFL (National Football
League) receivers.

The pass receiver is considered a "skilled" position. It
requires consistency, quickness, good hands, concentration,
and courage.

Pass receivers include wide receivers, tight ends, and
running backs. The wide receivers usually line up out to the
sides of their teammates. The running backs line up behind
and sometimes out to the sides of the quarterback. The tight
end lines up at one end of the offensive line.

Consistency

Consistency means that the receiver can be counted on to
catch the ball. Even the greatest receivers will drop an occa-
sional pass, but if they have consistency, the coach will
continue to play them. Consistency is more important than
speed. What good is a fast receiver if he doesn't catch the
ball?

Quickness

The most important physical asset is *quickness*. To be a receiver you must be able to change direction fast in order to separate yourself from a defender and get to the ball.

Good Hands

Good receivers catch every pass in their *hands*—not against their body. A good receiver needs "soft hands," meaning that he can catch and hold on to the football, no matter how hard, or where it is thrown. Those with "hard hands" seem to grab at the ball and struggle to control it with their fingertips.

You need a lot of practice catching the ball in order to learn the correct moves.

Concentration

Receivers must pay attention on every pass pattern. You can't allow defenders to force you from your pass route, and you must keep defenders from "stripping" (tearing) the ball from your hands as you catch it. You must also resist contact with tacklers. *Concentrate* on only three things: getting in the open to catch the ball, catching it, and holding on to it.

Courage

Courage is important to all football players, but the receiver must be especially courageous. Many times you will be off balance and unable to protect yourself when making the catch. You must hold onto the ball and be willing to take a hit. Don't worry if in the beginning you shy away and turn your head while making contact. If you are willing to master your fears, your courage will grow with practice.

Getting Ready to Run

Running a good pass pattern begins with the correct stance.

The Stance

Wide receivers use a *two-point stance*, meaning that they have two points of contact (their feet) with the ground. Stand with one foot slightly back, bend your knees, and lean forward (Figure 4-1). This stance is comfortable and simple. You can see everything from this position. This stance also helps you stay on your feet when you're bumped by a defender.

Tight ends use a *three-point stance*. You have three points of contact (your feet and one hand) with the ground. Place your feet a shoulder's width apart with one foot slightly back. Lean forward and place the fingertips of your right hand (left, for lefties) on the ground. Rest your other elbow on your knee. In this stance you can't see much and you may have trouble hearing the snap count, so the first thing you do when getting out of a three-point stance is to get into a two-point stance!

In either stance, be ready to shift your weight to your front foot so you can get a quick start at the snap of the ball.

4-1 WIDE RECEIVER'S STANCE: Wide receivers use a two-point stance, knees bent, weight slightly forward and head looking in for the snap. Hang your arms loosely at the sides and keep your upper body relaxed so you can execute a quick and explosive jump.

Checking Pass Coverage

The first thing a receiver looks for is whether the defensive coverage is man-for-man (each defensive player has to cover a specific offensive player) or zone (each defensive player has an area to cover). Before leaving the line of scrimmage, check the position of the three closest pass defenders. If you are lined up on the right, you should be able to see the cornerback, free safety, and first linebacker inside. If you're on the left, you can see the corner, strong safety and linebacker. With experience, you'll be able to get a good idea of their positions and coverage after the first three or four steps.

Things to Look For:

1. A defender playing man-for-man is more intense. He doesn't have time to drop into area coverage.

2. The kind of pass drops the linebackers are taking.

3. Check the defense. If there's a defender standing directly in your path, you'll have to get past him.

4. Don't stare at the defender who is covering you or whose zone you will enter.

5. Run the pattern as it was laid out in practice, but be ready to make on-the-move adjustments because of defensive traffic.

6. Separate from your defender as quickly as possible. This gives you time to make the catch without the defender trying to deflect the ball.

Pass Patterns

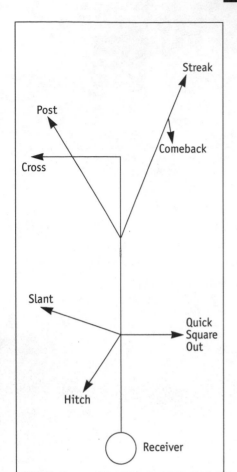

Here are six types of pass patterns:

1. **Outs.** The *quick square-out* is a five-yard pass thrown before you make your cut toward the sideline. The quarterback will throw the ball low and in front of you. You come back to catch the ball so the defender can't catch it. The *hitch* is similar to the square-out, except that you sprint five yards, then turn to face the quarterback without breaking toward the sideline.

2. **Slant.** You run through the defense on a *slant* (forty-five degree angle) and the quarterback throws the ball low.

3. **Comeback Patterns.** In a *comeback* pattern you run fifteen or twenty yards down the sidelines and jam on the brakes to drive the defender backward. Before the defender can recover, you run back toward the ball. A first cousin to the comeback is the hook, in which you look for an opening in the middle of the field between linebackers. When you find the opening, come back toward the quarterback, who throws the ball low, to protect it from the defender.

4. **Crossing Patterns.** On *crossing patterns*, you run fifteen to twenty yards downfield, then cut across the middle.

5. **Post Pattern.** In the *post* pattern, you start downfield, then break toward the goal post.

6. **Streak Pattern.** In the *streak* pattern, you run straight downfield.

Running Good Pass Patterns

Here are some moves that will help you run good pass patterns.

Pressure the Defender

Put *pressure* on the defender by closing in on him. When the ball is snapped, he'll move to the area he's supposed to protect. If it looks like he's moving outside, move with him, pressure him, then run your pattern.

Body Language

Use your *body language* to fake the defender until you reach the "top" of the pattern (the point where you make your move with a burst of speed). For example, you may be running a ten or twelve yard hook pattern. Within those ten or twelve yards, make the defender believe that you're going to run right past him.

Here's some body language techniques:

1. **Look the defender squarely in the eye.** This will make him nervous.

2. **Turn without straightening up.** Once you take off, the defender will be backpedaling. At the moment you straighten up to make your cut (turn), the defender will straighten up too, and he will start moving in on you. If you turn without straightening up, it will take more time for him to move in on you, leaving you in the clear to catch the ball.

3. **Put on a burst of speed.** Pump your arms as fast as you can while running, making the defender think that you're going deep (long) when you really plan to go no farther than ten or twelve yards.

4. **Change direction.** How fast you can run is not as important as how fast you can change direction. Defensive backs are usually fast, but you have the advantage of knowing where you are going. You act, causing the defensive backs to react. If you can get the back to hesitate, even for a split-second, you can get enough separation from him for you to receive a pass.

5. **Use your hips and shoulders.** Make the defender wonder when, and in what direction, you will make the cut. For example, if you run a five-yard slant down the field and intend to turn to the inside, turn your hips and shoulders as if you are turning to the outside, then quickly turn the other way.

Adjust on the Move

The defense will often be set up to interfere with your route so you must *adjust on the move*. For example, if you're running a hook pattern to the inside and the linebacker is moving into that space, hook well inside him or slide outside. Set up a plan and stick to it at all times. Your quarterback must be sure where you're heading or he may be sacked, or the ball may be intercepted (caught by a defensive player).

Find an Open Area

If you have to adjust, try to get into an *open area* where you can see the quarterback and he can see you. He will probably spot the open space and anticipate your coming into it.

Separation

Separation is the key to the passing game. If you are unable to put distance between yourself and the defender, he can try to intercept the ball. Two things are necessary to get away from him: you need a burst of speed, and the quarterback must throw the ball to the best separation point.

Catching the Ball

Here are some tips that will help you make good catches:

Outside the Lines

CATCHING

"UNCATCHABLE" PASSES

High Passes. Either grab the ball, or allow it to fall, then grab it.

Low Passes. Bend your legs. Form your hands and arms into a scoop, so you can scoop the ball into your body. If you have to dive, scoop while you're diving, then roll over on your shoulder, not your arms, to keep the ball from coming loose.

Passes Behind You. Slow down. Turn your hips toward the ball and reach back with both hands.

Passes in Front of You. Speed up. Try to reach past the ball and bring it in.

The Eyes Have It

One of the oldest rules in football is: The *eyes* catch the ball; the hands hold it. This means that you must "see" (actually watch) the ball hit your hands before closing your hands around it. If you take your eyes off the ball for even a split second, you're likely to miss the catch.

Catch the Black Dot Drill

This exercise will help train you to "see" the ball all the way into your hands. A large black dot is painted on the tip of the football. Another player throws the ball for you to catch. Concentrate on watching the black dot on the tip of the football as it comes toward you. Keep your concentration on the dot until the football is in your hands.

The Hands

A good pass is thrown "on the numbers," (aimed for the numbers on your jersey). If the quarterback's throw is off, you will have to adjust your *hands* for the catch.

Body Position

The prime rule about *body position* is to keep your body between the ball and the defender so he can't make an interception. If you run a streak pattern and must speed up or slow down, extend your arms to catch the ball. If you run a hook pattern and the ball is a little late, and the defender is coming at you from behind, make your body as big as possible by expanding your shoulders, lifting your arms, and raising up.

Tucking and Running

After you've caught the ball, you must secure it by *tucking* it away before *running* (Figures 4-2 to 4-4). If you get the ball when there are lots of defenders nearby, place your left hand (right, for lefties) over the point of the ball and your right hand (left, for lefties) over the ball itself. Move it into the football "carrying position," by putting the rear nose of the football under your far armpit. Tuck the elbow of that arm tight against your body and cup the front nose of the ball in the other hand.

If you are hemmed in by one or more tacklers, use one quick move to try and beat them. Be decisive, or the tacklers won't be fooled. If you miss, drive through them hard to get as much yardage as possible before being tackled. Always fall forward when tackled.

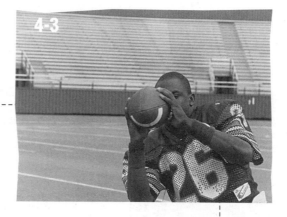

4-2 to 4-4 CATCHING THE BALL: Extend your arms and hands to catch the ball. Keep your eyes on the ball the entire way, until you see it enter your hands. After the ball is caught, tuck it away before running.

Blocking

In a game, there are usually more plays that require receivers to block than to catch passes. There are also pass plays that require you to block. Here are the two most effective blocks:

1. **The Stalk Block.** Come off the line of scrimmage fast and convince the defender that you're running a pattern, forcing him to backpedal. *Stalk* the defender by mirroring every move he makes until he moves to tackle the runner. Then shoulder block the defender by placing your head and shoulders across his path. If you block too early, the defender can avoid the block and make the tackle.

2. **The Cut Block.** This is a good change of pace if you have been using the stalk block. Act as if you are going to use the stock block again, then when you get within two yards of the defender, target his thigh pad and *cut* straight up and through the pad. This block requires perfect aim.

Lock on Drill

This is a blocking drill to practice making contact with the defender and "locking on" (keeping him from getting away from you).

You will be set up facing another player, who is the defender. On the coach's command, the defender moves in the direction he was assigned by the coach. Make contact with the defender and keep up the contact until the whistle blows.

Playing Defense

There will be times when the receiver must become a pass defender and keep the defense from intercepting the ball. The basic rule is: prevent an interception at all costs.

When you see a bad throw coming and know that you can't catch it, make sure the defender doesn't catch it either. Don't allow the defender to cut or jump in front of you. If the ball is up for grabs, be aggressive and play defense. Knock the ball away from him, knock him down, strip the ball, whatever it takes. To "strip" an interceptor, bring your arms down over him from behind, run your hands down his arms, pulling them apart and forcing them away from the ball. Remember that receiver and defender have the same rights when the ball is in the air. If the ball hits one of them and bounces in the air, both can do whatever it takes to legally prevent a catch or interception.

Make It Up, Play It Out

Here's an easy game that will give you and your friends lots of practice catching the ball.

Shuttle

You need four or more players, a football, and a field. Divide the players into two teams. Teams line up facing each other with the players lined up, one behind the other in a straight line. The first player on one team throws the football to the first player on the other team. The player that threw the ball, immediately runs to the back of his team's line and the next player moves forward to take his place.

The first player on the other team who catches the ball, throws it back to the other team's new, front player, who catches it and throws it back to the other team's new, front player. Players keep shifting position and catching and throwing the ball until someone misses. The player who misses is eliminated. Play continues until there is one player left, and his team is the winner.

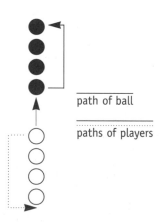

path of ball

paths of players

Seven Steps to Being a Good Receiver

1. Get off the line of scrimmage.
2. Run your assigned route.
3. Adjust to the defense.
4. Beat the defender.
5. Catch the football.
6. Tuck it away securely.
7. Run with the ball.

Q **A** *Were you surprised that you became a starter your rookie year and that you did so well?*

I know that coaches are concerned because any rookie quarterback's performance is going to be unpredictable. But once I got the starting job, they told me I had the talent to perform more like a veteran than a rookie. So whatever success I was able to achieve was somewhat of a pleasant surprise, but not totally unexpected.

Q **A** *Is there one particular talent you feel that has helped you in particular?*

I have had good coaching going all the way back to my high school days. At Penn State, my coaches taught me to always be in control and how to make good decisions.

Q **A** *How fast do you think you can develop into a competent and effective NFL quarterback?*

I'm not sure, but I know it depends on no one other than myself. The coaches here have been great and haven't put any undo pressure on me to develop my game any faster than is comfortable for me. They've explained to me that I'm bound to make mistakes as I go along, but as long as I show the ability to learn from my mistakes and not to repeat them, I'll have a good future in the NFL.

Q **A** *Which physical characteristic do you feel has contributed the most to your success?*

At six feet, six inches and 240 pounds, I'm bigger than some of the guys who try to tackle me. This makes it a little more difficult to bring me down in the pocket or in the open field, which buys me a few extra second to find an open receiver and complete a pass or to get rid of the ball and not take a loss.

Q **A** *Were there any games in particular during your rookie season that stand out?*

During our game with the New England Patriots there were two passes I called at the line of scrimmage when I saw the defense preparing to blitz. Both of them resulted in touchdowns and we went on to win in overtime.

CHAPTER 5

Offensive Linemen

The offensive linemen do the heavy work on every play. They push defenders out of the way long enough for a running back to get through, and they keep defenders away from the quarterback long enough for him to throw the ball. Offensive linemen are also known as "blockers," because they block the path of the defenders. To gain the strength needed to do their job, offensive linemen work out with weights on a regular basis. Offensive linemen work very hard and don't get as much glory as the quarterbacks and running backs, but quarterbacks and running backs would not be stars without their linemen.

There are five offensive linemen: two guards, two tackles, and one center. All five offensive linemen think and play as one. Their success depends on a combined effort in which each player does his job.

Guards and Tackles

Guards and tackles set up at the line of scrimmage and about a yard back from the ball. There will be one guard and one

tackle to the right of the center, and one guard and one tackle to the left of the center.

Guards and tackles use a balanced stance so they can explode into action when the ball is snapped (put into play).

Hands

The offensive lineman's hands must be strong and fast. You must be able to push a defender and get him moving backward so he can't get to the ball carrier.

The Stance for Guards and Tackles

To make sure your body will be lined up correctly, do the following (Figure 5-1):

1. **Set your feet parallel to each other** with one foot slightly behind the other one.

2. **Place the fingertips of your right hand** (left for lefties) on the ground directly under your shoulder and out in front of your back foot. There should be a space of six to eight inches between your elbow and your knee. Lay your other arm across your thigh and loosely clench the fist.

3. **Distribute your weight equally** among your feet and the hand that touches the ground. Be aware of which foot you will use to make your move, but don't lean in that direction or you will tip the defense off to your plan.

4. **Your back should be parallel to the ground,** but if your butt is a little higher than your shoulders, that's all right, too.

5. **Hold your head in a comfortable position.** You should be able to see no farther than the feet of the man five yards away.

6. **Keep your knees in line with your feet and hips.** This will provide maximum power from your legs.

Take Off

Once you are in the correct stance, wait for the ball to be snapped, then take off. Here's how:

1. **Take a short, six-inch step** in the direction of the play.

2. **Make your second step very quick** and in line with the defender you will be blocking. (There is more on how to block later in this chapter.)

5-1 STANCE: Keep your back parallel to the ground and your butt slightly higher than the shoulders. Balance your weight, place your lead hand (touching the ground) on your fingertips, 6–8 inches from the knee and in front of the back foot. Rest your other arm across the thigh. Place one foot just ahead of the other, feet parallel. Keep your head and eyes looking straight ahead.

The Center

The center lines up right behind the ball, in the middle of the offensive line. His job is to snap (deliver) the ball to the quarterback, then block defenders, just like the guards and tackles.

The Stance for the Center

Here's how you set up (Figure 5-2):

1. **Set your feet parallel to each other** and as far apart as your shoulders.

2. **Lean forward over the ball and grip it** with your right hand (left for lefties). The ball should be almost directly under your right eye (under the left eye for lefties) with the laces up. Grip the ball near the tip with your thumb on one side of the laces and the rest of your fingers on the other side of the laces, forming a V over the laces.

3. **Place the fingers of your left hand** (right for lefties) on the ground even with the back of the ball and directly in front of your knee.

4. **Raise your head** so you can see the linebacker's feet, about three yards away.

5. **Make sure your butt is almost even with your head.**

Snap the Ball

When you *snap* the ball, pass it up through your legs and into the quarterback's hands, which will be resting on your butt (Figure 5-3). Before you snap the ball, be aware of the pressure of the quarterback's hands on your butt, so you know exactly where to place the ball. Before snapping the ball, center it on a straight line between your legs.

Keep your back flat as the ball is snapped. Don't dip your head.

Release the ball the instant it hits the quarterback's hands. It is now his responsibility to secure the ball. You want to make the snap and go right into a block.

5-2 CENTER STANCE: Place your feet shoulder-width apart, knees turned out directly over the feet. Toes are parallel. The head is raised and the ball is out front, just centered off the body line. Grip the ball with the forefinger and thumb of the lead hand, forming a V along the ball's seam. Place the other hand on the thigh so you can quickly get into a blocking position.

5-3 CENTER SNAP: The ball should be lifted directly into the quarterback's hands with a natural elbow motion. The center needs to be aware of where the quarterback's hands are before he snaps the ball.

Types of Blocks

Blocking requires great strength and quickness. You need to be able to stay on your feet while fending off pass rushers (defenders that are going after the ball carrier). There are five basic blocks.

Drive Block

The *drive block* is also known as the "base block." You will be driving against a defender while he is driving against you (Figure 5-4). You will want to use this basic block most of the time.

1. **Drive off your stance** with your "up," or front foot, then step forward about six inches with your back foot. Take a second step with the "up" foot. Don't make this a very big step or you might lose your balance.

2. **Take aim.** If the defender is in a stance, aim for the numbers. If the defender is in the stand-up position, target his belt buckle.

3. **Make contact with your forearms.** It helps if you thrust your hips up and under you as you make contact.

4. **Don't lose your balance.** Keep your feet beneath your armpits as you drive the defender.

5. **Stay lower than the defender.**

6. **Keep blocking until you hear the whistle** (meaning the play is over).

Double Team Block

In the *double team block*, two linemen work together to block one defender (Figures 5-5 and 5-6). This block is also known as the "power block." In this block, one lineman is the "post" man and the other lineman is the "lead" man. The post and lead players block side-by-side.

The Post Player

The *post* man's job is to stop the defender's charge and give the lead man an opening to go for the defender's hip.

1. Aim for the defender "at the numbers" (the numbers on his jersey), and block him in the center of his body.

2. Get under the defender regardless of how low he goes. Stop his charge and lift him up as much as possible.

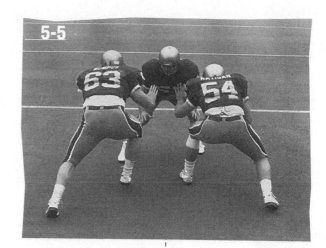

5-4 DRIVE OR BASE BLOCK: Make initial contact with the outside of your forearms, drive with your legs.

The Lead Player

The *lead* man's job is to finish off the block.

1. Come out of your stance and make contact with the defender in the area from his chest to his hips.

2. Be careful not to knock the post man off balance.

5-5 and 5-6 DOUBLE TEAM BLOCK: When you and your teammate double team the defender or "power block," attack the defender as close to the center of his body as possible (player's numbers or chinstrap).

The post man and the lead man must always be prepared to switch roles. If the defender should slant toward the lead man, then the lead man becomes the post man, and the post man becomes the lead man.

Fold Block

Another type of block that uses two linemen is the *fold block*. One offensive lineman blocks a defensive lineman, while the second offensive lineman crosses behind his teammate to get the linebacker.

Pass Block

In a *pass block* (Figure 5-7), you must hold off the pass rusher for however long it takes for the quarterback to complete the play (usually from three to six seconds). Stay between the pass rusher and the quarterback. The pass rusher will make contact with you. You must tie up the pass rusher (keep him busy) so he can't get to the quarterback. Keep your arms extended and keep your feet moving, picking them up and down in quick steps. Work to keep the pass rusher at the line of scrimmage.

5-7 PASS BLOCK: The pass blocker must try to mirror the rusher's moves like he's defending man-to-man.

Trap Block

The *trap block* is a trick play designed to fool the defense into thinking that your running back will be coming up one side of the field when he will really be coming up the other side.

The trap block is used by a guard. Imagine that you're the left guard. After the snap, you step behind the center and pull out to the right so that you can contact your designed (assigned to you in the huddle) defender over on the right side of the field. Now you're an extra blocker on the right side of the field and you can provide extra protection for the running back.

Allow the defender to penetrate, then make contact and drive him backward by thrusting with your feet, legs, and hips.

You need to run this play very fast because there may be an unguarded defender on the loose who can "sack" the quarterback or go after the running back. A sack is when the quarterback is tackled behind the line of scrimmage while he still has the ball, for a loss of yardage.

No matter which defender you have been assigned to block, never let an unblocked defender get by you.

Push-Pull Drill

This drill will help you learn to keep your balance while blocking. You will be facing another player, who is the defender. The defender begins the drill by grabbing your shoulders. On the coach's command, the defender tries to turn your shoulders, pull you forward, or push you back. Resist the defender by keeping your fists together on your chest with your elbows out to your sides. Move your feet to keep your balance. Keep resisting until the coach blows the whistle.

Eight Steps to Making a Good Block

1. Know your assignment.
2. Start with a comfortable stance.
3. Use three steps to drive into action: a drive off the "up" foot, a six-inch step with the other foot, and a third step with the first foot.
4. Make contact with the outside of your forearms, aiming at the defender's numbers if he is in a stance, or his belt buckle if he is standing up.
5. Thrust your hips up and under the defender while bringing your feet into position.
6. Drive the defender by staying lower than him.
7. Follow through and finish the man off.
8. Don't stop until the whistle blows.

6

Defense

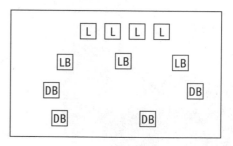

The job of the defense is to stop the other team's offense from moving the ball toward their goal. One way to stop them is by tackling the ball carrier (knocking him down). The defense also tries to get the ball away from the offense.

To play for the defense you have to be able to make good tackles. You also need to think fast. When the offensive players come to the line of scrimmage, they already have a plan for the play. Since you don't know what that plan is, you have to be ready for anything!

The eleven members of the defensive team include the *linemen*, the *linebackers*, and the *defensive backs*. The linemen play up front on the line of scrimmage. The linebackers play behind the linemen, and the defensive backs play in the defensive backfield (behind the linebackers and out to the sides).

Basic Formations

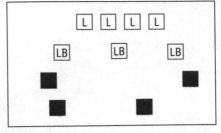

Here are some basic formations (ways of lining up) that are used by the defensive team:

The Four-Man Line

The *four-man line* is also called the *four-three* because there are four defensive linemen on the line of scrimmage and three linebackers away from the line.

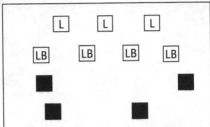

The Three-Man Line

The *three-man line* is also called the *three-four* because there are three defensive linemen on the line of scrimmage and four linebackers away from the line.

Tackling

All defensive players need to know how to tackle (knock down your opponent). Whenever you make a tackle you should stay in the "spirit of the game," meaning that you should go all-out to knock down blockers or tackle the ball carrier, but you should never play "dirty" (try to hurt them on purpose) (Figure 6-1).

If you follow the rules for making a good tackle, you'll bring down the runner and avoid getting hurt. Always follow these two rules:

1. **Never use your helmet as a weapon.** The head and neck are easily injured when a tackler drives his head into the offensive player's body. This is illegal and it can seriously hurt both players.

2. **Don't arm tackle.** Arm tackling means using just your shoulders and arms to make a tackle. You can get hurt that way. You need to tackle with your whole body.

6-1 TACKLING ONE-ON-ONE: Lead with your torso into the ball carrier on a lower plane, wrap his arms, and drive his hips and body up through the jersey number. Keep your arms wrapped and legs moving until the play is finished. Notice the head (helmet) is not used as a weapon.

Playing by the Rules

In addition to the two basic rules listed above, you are not allowed to:

- Kick or knee an opponent.
- Trip an opponent.
- Hit an opponent's face, head, or neck with your hand, forearm, or elbow.
- Grab an opponent's face mask.
- Block or tackle anyone after the ball is dead.

Tackling Straight On

Drive into him, *straight on*. Use your chest against his body. Wrap your arms around the offensive player and lift. The force of your body along with the lifting motion will put him on the ground.

Tackling in the Open Field

When both you and your target (the ball carrier or pass receiver) are in the open, make sure that you're balanced and can move with him. On contact, drive right through him, putting your chest against his jersey number. Wrap your arms around him, lift him up, and he'll go down.

Tackling on an Angle

Most tackles happen when you are coming at an angle to the ball carrier. Here's how to make a good tackle on an angle:

1. **Get your chest on his outside number** (the number on his jersey that's closest to the sideline).
2. **Try to stay lower than he is.**
3. **Drive your hips and chest** up through his outside number as if you were taking your body to a point five yards beyond him. It's important that your momentum (forward force) be stronger than his.
4. **Wrap your arms around** the lower part of his body, and continue to drive him to the ground. Your head will end up in front of him, and your body will take the force of the tackle.

Defensive Linemen

Defensive lineman play right up front on the line of scrimmage. When you're a defensive lineman, you're in the middle of

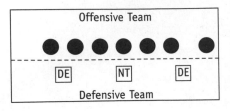

Offensive Team

DE NT DE

Defensive Team

everything. Your job is to take on an offensive lineman and hold him or push him back. You need to move as soon as the ball is snapped (handed off by the center). If a blocker from the other team gets to you before you move forward, you're probably not going to be able to hold him. You need to be strong enough to handle being "double-teamed" (hit by two blockers at once).

One kind of defensive lineman is the *defensive end*. The ends try to come around the outside of the offensive tackles and go after the quarterback. When one defensive lineman lines up facing the other team's center, that lineman is called the *nose tackle*.

Setting Up

There are two basic stances for defensive linemen, the three-point stance and the four-point stance.

The Three-Point Stance

The *three-point stance* is used by most defensive ends. In the three-point stance, you have three points of contact with the ground, your two feet and one hand (Figure 6-2). Getting down on one hand helps you make a lower charge, and in a battle with a blocker, the lowest man wins.

To get into a three-point stance:

1. **Set your feet a shoulder's width apart and parallel to each other,** with one foot slightly behind the other one.

2. **Place the fingertips of your right hand** (left for lefties) on the ground under your shoulder and in front of your back foot.

3. **Rest most of your weight** on your hand and back foot, and raise your heels a little off the ground.

5. **Bend your knees a bit** so your back is parallel to the ground.

4. **Keep your head up.** Look the blocker in the eye.

6-2 THREE-POINT STANCE: Keep your head up and eyes focused on the blocker's eyes, weight resting on the upfield hand and leg. Place your feet shoulder-width apart and get your tail slightly higher than your shoulders.

6-3 FOUR-POINT STANCE: Extend both arms, weight evenly placed on each hand, fingertips extended. Keep your shoulders parallel to the line of scrimmage, back slightly inclined toward the front, knees bent, feet parallel and shoulder-width apart.

The Four-Point Stance

The *four-point stance* is used most often by the nose tackle (Figure 6-3). The nose tackle is likely to have to fight off a double-team block, so he needs to stay low in order to get all the power he can. The four-point stance is also used by other linemen when they need to get a really low charge.

To get into a four-point stance:

1. **Set your feet a shoulder's width apart and parallel to each other.**
2. Bend over and **place the fingertips of both hands** on the ground directly under your shoulders.
3. **Bend your knees a bit** so your back is parallel to the ground.
4. **Raise your heels a little off the ground.**
5. **Keep your head up** so you can watch the offensive players.

Charge!

Defensive linemen use a variety of *charges*, or "stunts," in order to get past the offensive blockers and get to the quarterback. These stunt charges confuse the offensive blockers and can cause them to mess up their assignments (the plan they were told to follow in the huddle). Three of the most commonly used stunts are: the slant, the loop, and shoot-the-gap.

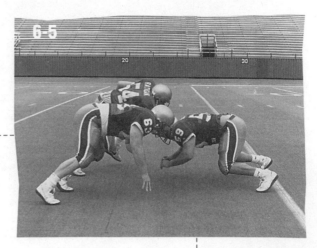

6-4 to 6-6 GOAL LINE AND SHORT YARDAGE STANCE: This is the same as the four-point stance except the arms and knees are bent slightly putting the body on a lower plane. When the ball is snapped, make a low charge and get into the gap between the offensive linemen. You need to be especially quick and explosive from this position.

Goal Line and Short Yardage

When the defense expects one of the running backs or the quarterback to carry the ball into the line you set up in a defensive stance designed to stop the run for little or no gain. Situations when this is likely to happen are if only a few yards are needed for a first down, or if the offense has the ball close to your end zone. (Figures 6-4 to 6-6.)

The Slant

Charge the offensive player on a *slant*, either to the left or the right. On your first step, aim at the far shoulder of the blocker. On your second step, get your foot past the blocker. Then look for the ball and move toward it (Figures 6-7 to 6-9).

The Loop

The purpose of this charge is to get past the blocker by *looping* around the outside of him. Start by taking a sideways step with

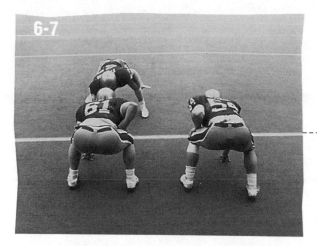

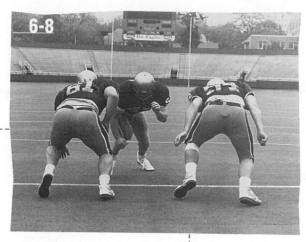

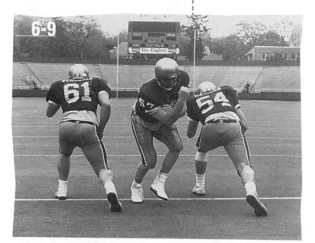

6-7 to 6-9 SLANT TECHNIQUE: Line up on the head of one of the two blockers. When the ball is snapped, move in a slanting motion into the gap between them, then look for the ball.

one foot. Without moving forward, cross your other foot over the first foot to carry you sideways even farther. On your next step, get your foot past the blocker, then look for the ball and move toward it.

Shoot-the-Gap

After you've been using the slant and loop charges, the blockers will be looking for you to try them again. Now's a good time to change your style and *shoot-the-gap*. This is a very quick charge that takes you through the gap (space) between blockers. Start this charge by stepping into the gap on a forty-five degree angle and getting one foot past the blocker. Use your arm and shoulder to protect that foot and hip. Look for the ball and move toward it.

Shed Drill

This drill teaches defensive linemen how to use their hands to defeat blockers.

Line up opposite another player who takes the part of an offensive lineman. On the coach's signal, the offensive player tries to drive his helmet past your left side and knock you off the line of scrimmage. React to him by moving to your left and making contact with your hands on his numbers. Then try to escape him.

Sack the Quarterback!

Rushing the passer (charging after the quarterback) and then *sacking* him is the best part of the defensive lineman's job.

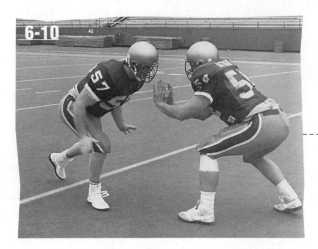

6-10 and 6-11 PASS RUSH: Start in the three-point stance and use your outside leg to explode through the shoulder of the offensive lineman, ripping your inside arm underneath the blocker's arm.

Sacking means to tackle the quarterback behind the line of scrimmage while he still has the ball. When you sack the quarterback, you end the play behind the line of scrimmage. You've pushed the offense back, causing then to loose yardage and making it harder for them to score.

The length of time you have to reach the quarterback before he throws the ball will depend on how far backward he runs before throwing. The offensive players will be forming a protective pocket (ring) around the quarterback to keep him from being sacked. Here are two ways to get through the blockers and get to the quarterback:

Pass Rush

The three point stance enables defensive lineman to get a better take off at the snap of the ball. You should think about getting to the passer first and then react to the run if the passer takes off or hands the ball to a running back. Keep after the blocker so that he is forced to backpedal uncontrollably which will put him off balance. Keep pushing toward the quarterback. When making contact with the quarterback, wrap up his arms before he can throw. If the quarterback is able to throw the ball before contact, get your arms and hands up in order to disrupt his vision. (Figures 6-10 and 6-11.)

Swim

Grab the blocker's jersey just inside the armpit. Swing around the blocker and make an overhand, *swimming* motion with your other arm. When you bring your arm down, use your shoulder and arm muscles to help you raise yourself up and over the blocker's arm and body. Once you are past the blocker, you will be free to rush the quarterback.

Rip

With your inside arm (closest to the blocker), make contact with the blocker's shoulder pad as if you are going to *rip* (drive) your arm right through the pad. Keep driving your body toward the outside of the blocker and use your "rip arm" to push the blocker back toward the quarterback. Move past the blocker and toward the quarterback.

Linebackers

Behind the linemen are the *linebackers*. Because the linemen are often busy "tying up" (blocking) the offensive blockers, linebackers are the players that make the most tackles.

The linebackers have one of the hardest jobs on the defensive team. Just like linemen, the linebackers have to get past offensive blockers and then rush the passer (quarterback). They must also be able to cover (stay with) the pass receivers and tackle them if they catch the ball. Linebackers stop the other team from making touchdowns.

Linebackers work out with weights to develop upper body and arm strength. Their arms must wrap around the ball carrier and hold on to him while putting him on the ground. Linebackers also need strong legs to help drive their body into the ball carrier with enough force to make the tackle.

Setting Up

Linebackers line up on the field behind the linemen. Linebackers can be known by different names, depending on where they set up. The *middle linebacker* is in the middle and plays opposite the offensive center. The *strong side linebacker* plays at the end of the line, opposite the offensive team's tight end. The *weak side linebacker* plays at the other end of the line, and the *inside linebackers* play inside the weak side and strong side linebackers.

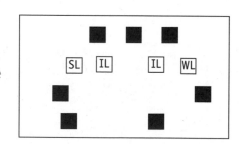

6-12 LINEBACKER'S STANCE: Take a square, semi-crouched position, feet parallel, head up, and arms hanging loosely in front and over the knees. Your weight should be held forward and one the balls of

The Stance

Set your feet a little wider apart than your shoulders and parallel to each other. Lean forward, bend your knees, and let your arms hang down so that your elbows are a little higher than your knees. Keep your weight on the front part of your feet so you are ready to spring forward (Figure 6-12).

Zone or Man-to-Man?

Whenever you come out on the field to play defense, the coach will have called for either *zone* coverage or *man-to-man* coverage.

Zone coverage means that you cover your assigned area of the field. Until a pass is thrown, don't follow a receiver out of your zone because that means that another receiver can come into your area and they won't be covered. After a pass is thrown, you can leave your area to tackle the ball carrier.

Man-to-man coverage means that you are assigned to cover a certain offensive player. Stick with him wherever he goes and tackle him if he catches a pass.

Making the Tackle

When you make a tackle, follow the rules and tips you read earlier in this chapter about tackling.

The Defensive Backs

Behind the linebackers and out to the sides of the linemen are another group of defensive players known as the *defensive backs*. The defensive backs are also known as the "secondary," because they play behind the other defensive players.

Defensive backs are great athletes. They have to be because they run backward a lot of the time. They need to able to change direction, and start and stop very quickly. They also need to be able to leap, because sometimes they will have to get up in the air to knock a ball away from a receiver or intercept a pass.

The defensive backs are also known as cornerbacks and safeties.

Cornerbacks

There are two *cornerbacks* and they line up at the corners of the defensive formation. The cornerbacks' job is to cover the offensive team's wide receivers. If the quarterback throws a long pass, he will most likely throw it to a wide receiver. As a cornerback, your assignment is to stay with the wide receiver and tackle him as soon as he catches the ball. If you fail in your assignment, the wide receiver could keep going to the end zone for a touchdown.

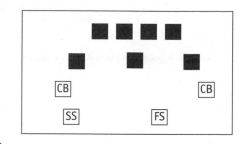

Safeties

The *safeties* line up behind the linebackers.

The *free safety* is free to roam around the backfield. He can go from the middle of the field to either sideline. His job is to help whichever cornerback is covering the pass receiver.

The *strong safety* sets up in the backfield, opposite the offensive team's tight end.

Backpedaling

All cornerbacks and safeties must have the ability to sprint in reverse while covering a potential receiver on the offense. This backpedal movement should have a smooth, fluid style with feet close to the ground which allows the defensive back to maintain both balance and rhythm. After moving backward for about 10 to 12 yards with short, choppy steps, you have to be able to turn and accelerate quickly into a sprint in order to stay with the receiver as he speeds down the field trying to catch a pass. (Figures 6-13 and 6-14.)

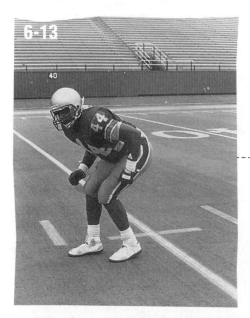

6-13 and 6-14 BACKPEDAL TECHNIQUE: Stand with your arms hanging loosely, body in a slight crouch, eyes looking at the ball. Begin backpedal technique by stepping backward, keeping feet close to the ground and under your body. Keep your body bent forward and move your arms in a back-and-forth motion.

Backpedal Drill

This drill gives defensive backs practice in backpedaling.
Two defensive backs are on the sideline, each one standing on a yard line with their back to the field. When the coach gives the signal, they backpedal across the yard line, while watching the coach. When the coach points out a direction, the backs break off backpedaling and run in that direction.

The Stance

Stand with your legs about a shoulder's width apart. Bend your knees and lean forward a bit. Let your arms hang loosely at your sides. If you're a cornerback, one foot should be a little farther back than the other. If you're a safety, stand with your body at a forty-five degree angle to the line of scrimmage.

Zone or Man-to-Man?

If you have been assigned to cover a *zone*, then cover any offensive players in your zone, and tackle the runner (ball carrier) if he comes into your zone.

If you are assigned *man-to-man* coverage, stay with your assigned receiver, and watch him for signs that he might be going to catch a pass. (If you keep your eyes on the ball or on the quarterback, you might miss a chance to intercept the pass, or tackle the receiver.) "Mirror" the receiver by running the same route that he does, except that you will be running backward so you can watch him.

When the receiver starts to look upward with his eyes, or if he starts to reach up, that tells you the ball is coming. Go after the ball by leaping for it to catch it high in the air. If you catch the ball, you've just made one of the biggest plays in football—an interception! Run with the ball toward your goal line. Maybe you will get all the way to the end zone and score a touchdown!

If you can't catch the ball, then try to knock it away so that the receiver can't catch it either.

If the receiver catches the ball, and you are positioned behind him, try to "strip" (knock loose) the ball by raising your arms above your and his head, and bringing them down around him (Figures 6-15 and

6-15 to 6-16 STRIPPING THE BALL: Come in behind the receiver and make contact by bringing your arms up over top. Then pull down, back, and out forcing the ball to fall free.

6-16). As you bring your arms down, keep your hands inside his arms to force them apart, causing him to drop the ball.

If you can't strip the ball, tackle the receiver to stop him from moving toward the goal line.

Making the Tackle

When you make a tackle, follow the rules and tips you read earlier in this chapter about tackling.

Make It Up, Play It Out

The game of Target Rush, will help sharpen your defense skills.

Target Rush

You need at least two players, a football, a target, and a field. One player is the defense and the other player is the offense. Let's say that you are the defense. Get set up at one end of the field near the target. The offensive player starts at the other end of the field. Yell, "Go!" to start the game. The offensive player may run with the ball to the target, or throw the ball at the target. If you tag him before he can reach the target, or if his throw misses the target, the play is over. He has four downs to hit the target. Start each down with the two players at the opposite ends of the field. After four downs, switch positions, so your friend can practice defense, too. The first player to hit the target ten times is the winner.

Keep Focused

1. When you make a tackle, go all-out. Don't merely "hit" the offensive player, use enough force to put him down.
2. Never play to hurt another player.
3. Never use your helmet as a weapon.
4. Don't arm tackle. Use your whole body.
5. When covering an offensive player, stick with him wherever he goes.
6. On running plays, try to strip the ball from the ball carrier as you tackle him.
7. On passing plays, try to catch the ball before the receiver can. Then run it toward your goal.

CHAPTER 7

The Kicking Game

Imagine that the game is almost over. Your team is behind by two points and there's just enough time left for one more play. A "field goal" (the ball is kicked high in the air and through the goal posts) is worth three points. You come on the field to kick for your team. If you make the kick, your team wins. If you miss, your team loses.

Kicking is such an important part of the game that each football team has smaller, "special teams" of kicking experts, just for the kicking plays.

There are two kinds of these special teams: the kicking team and the kick return team.

The Kicking Team

The kicking team can include the center, the holder, the kicker, and blockers. There are three kinds of kicks: the kickoff, place-kicking, and punting.

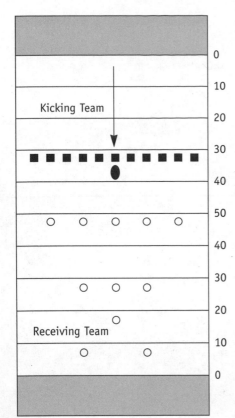

Kicking Team

Receiving Team

The Kickoff

The football is put into play at the start of each half with a *kickoff*. Before the game begins, the referee tosses a coin to determine which team will kick off first. The team that does not kick off at the beginning of the game will kick off to start the second half. The kickoff is also used to put the ball into play after a touchdown or a field goal has been scored.

The ball is placed on a tee (ball holder) on the forty-yard line of the kicking team. The kicker runs toward the ball and kicks it as far as he can into the other team's territory. The receiving team catches the ball and runs it back up the field as far as they can.

Place-kicking

Place-kicking means that the ball is held in place by the holder, while the kicker kicks it. Place-kicking is a three-man job. The center, the holder, and the kicker all work together (Figures 7-1 to 7-6).

The Center

The *center's* job is to snap the ball to the holder. To snap the ball correctly, pick it up from the line of scrimmage, hold it in both hands, and snap (toss) it backwards between your legs at the holder's hands.

It's not so easy to hit your target (the holder's hands) when you're looking backwards and upside down. Getting the hang of it takes lots of practice.

Once you've snapped the ball, straighten up so that you can block any defenders that are rushing (coming after) the kicker.

The Holder

The *holder* is always a player that is used to handling the football. The holder might be a quarterback, a receiver, or a defensive back.

To hold the ball, you must first set up in the correct position. Face the sideline, and bend your knee that is closest to the kicker. Kneel down on your other knee. Twist your body a bit so that you're facing the center. Stretch out your arms to catch the ball.

When you've caught the ball, twist back to face the sideline and spin the ball so that the laces are pointing toward the goal posts (away from the kicker). Place the ball about six inches out in front of your foot that is nearest the kicker. Now put the index (pointer) finger of your right hand (left for lefties) on the tip of the ball and hold it in place while the kicker runs up and kicks the ball out from under your finger.

At first, you might be worried about getting your finger or hand kicked. That's okay. The fear will go away with practice.

The Kicker

Here's how you make a good kick:

1. **Line up two steps behind the ball** and off to one side at about a forty-five degree angle to the ball.
2. **Place your left foot** slightly ahead of the right, with most of the weight on your front foot .
3. **Keep your head down,** and watch the ball from the moment it leaves the center's hands until it is placed by the holder.
4. **Take a short step forward** with your kicking foot. Then plant (place) your non-kicking foot so that it points directly at the ball. This will force you to pivot your body to face the goal post. Your planted foot should be about eight to ten inches from the ball.
5. **Bring your kicking leg back,** and as you bring it down to kick the ball, lean slightly away from the ball. You should strike the ball with the inside of your foot.
6. **Follow through** after the ball has been kicked by continuing the upward motion of your leg.

Kicking Drill

Pick out six spots on the field near the goal post. Another player holds the ball on the first spot. Try to kick the ball between the uprights of the goal post. Practice until you make a good kick, then move on to the next spot and try for another field goal. Keep practicing until you get a field goal from every spot. Then you can be the holder and the other player can be the kicker.

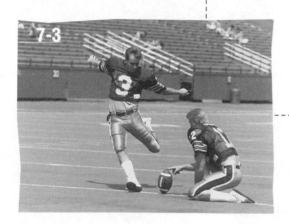

7-1 to 7-6 PLACE-KICKING: Keep your eyes glued to the ball and the spot where the holder will place it (about two steps away) before the approach. Begin your approach by leaning forward, transferring your weight to your front foot and then taking your first step with your rear foot. Plant your non-kicking foot and begin sweep through with your kicking foot. Strike the ball with the top part of your instep and drive through the ball. Keep your head down throughout. If you are the holder, kneel with the leg closest to the end zone bent beneath you and the other leg bent at the knee. Keep your arms are fully extended and hands toward the center to receive the ball. Look at the spot where the ball will be placed before putting it down, spin it so the laces face the goalposts, and secure it with one finger.

Punting

Punting is used when your team has failed to get a first down (gain ten yards) in three plays. If you should fail to get a first down on the fourth play, the other team gets the ball. You want the other team to get the ball as far away from their goal line as possible, so you *punt*, or kick the ball as far into their territory as you can (Figures 7-7 to 7-12).

Punting is also known as drop-kicking because the kicker holds the ball in his hands, drops it into the air, and kicks it.

Here's how to kick a successful punt:

1. **Watch the ball until it is in your hands.**
2. **Catch the ball with both hands** in front of your chest with your arms outstretched.
4. **Hold the ball firmly while taking one step forward.**
5. On your second step, **drop the ball.**
6. Bring your kicking foot back, then forward to **kick the ball.**
7. **Kick the ball with the top of your foot** (the area just above your toes). You should make contact with the ball at about knee level.
8. **Follow through** on your kick by bringing your leg all the way up to the level of your shoulder.

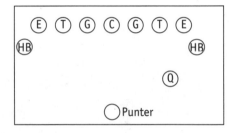

7-7 to 7-12 PUNTING THE BALL: Reach for the ball when it's snapped to receive it as soon as possible. As you begin your first step, drop the ball from the mid-point of your body in line with the anticipated arc or swing of your punting foot. The ball needs to be dropped far enough from the body so that you can extend your leg in your kicking motion. As the ball descends it should be level and angled a few inches toward the supporting foot. After planting the non-kicking foot, make contact with the punting foot with the ball slightly below the knee level. Swing through an upward arc. The follow-through should bring your kicking foot beyond the top of your head.

The Kick Return Team

When a ball is kicked into your territory by your opponent, you want to get the ball and run it back up the field as far as you can. The special team for returning kickoffs and punts is made up of players who can catch the ball, who are fast, and who can make sharp cuts in order to get away from players on the kicking team who are rushing them.

Returning the Punt

In order to *return the punt*, you must concentrate on first catching the ball, even though you are in danger of being tackled. If you don't make the catch, the other team may be able to get the ball back. You need to know where your blockers are, and where there is an open space to run the ball upfield. Once you've caught the ball, run it up the field, making cuts in order to help your blockers protect you, and to avoid being tackled.

The Fair Catch

In cases when you are able to make the catch but won't be able to run the ball upfield, raise your arm straight up into the air before you catch the ball to signal a *fair catch* (Figures 7-13 and 7-14). The other team will see your signal and must allow you to catch the ball without being tackled. When you signal a fair catch, you have to catch the ball and stay put. You can not try to run the ball upfield.

7-13 and 7-14 FAIR CATCH: You must get to the spot where the ball will land and then, sometimes with the help of your co-safetyman, determine that you can't return it. Signal by waving your right arm, continuing that action while getting into position to make a clean "fair catch."

Leaving the Ball Untouched

If you know that you won't be able to catch the ball without being tackled, or if you stumble before you catch the ball, *do not touch the ball*. If you touch the ball and then loose it, the other team is allowed to recover (take back) the ball.

Returning the Kickoff

When returning a kickoff, there are no fair catches. If the receiver can catch the ball, he has to return it up the field. However, if you see that the ball is going to go out of bounds, let it go. If the ball goes out of bounds, the kickoff team will get a penalty or will have to rekick.

Make It Up, Play It Out

Here's a game for two or more players that will sharpen your kick return skills:

Kick Return

You need a football, kicker's tee, and a field. To start the game the football should be set up in the kicker's tee. One person is the kicker and the other person is the receiver. The receiver takes his position at one end of the field. The kicker kicks the ball toward the receiver. The receiver catches the ball and tries to run past the tee. The kicker tries to stop him by touching him with both hands. If the receiver gets past the tee, he gets a point. Players take turns kicking the ball. The first player to get seven points is the winner.

If things go wrong with your kick, here's a checklist to help you figure out what the problem is:

1. Your kicks are too short. The laces of the football may be facing you, or your planted foot might be too far ahead of the ball, or you may be forgetting to follow through.
2. You're kicking too far to the right. If you're a right-handed kicker, your planted foot may be too far from the ball, or pointing to the outside.
3. You're kicking too far to the left. Your planted foot may be too close to the ball.
4. Your kicks are too low. Your foot may be hitting the ball too high, or your planted foot may be pointing to the outside.

8

The Game Plan

F ootball is a bit like checkers, chess, and some other board games, because you have a better chance of winning if you figure out your strategy (plan of attack) before the first move is made. In football, that strategy is called the game plan.

Coming up with the *game plan* is a part of the coach's job. He must decide on what plays are most likely to work best for his players, and then include those plays in his plan. Then he must make sure that his players all understand the plan and practice the plays.

Making the Game Plan

When the coach chooses a game plan, he uses any information he has on the opposing team and what he knows about his own team.

College Level

In *college football*, the coaches gather as much information as possible on the team they will play against. One way they do this it to watch videos of the other team in action (past games). They watch the videos several times, to see what each player's strengths and weaknesses are. They also watch to see which plays the other team uses most. Do they throw more passes or use more running plays? Which pass patterns? Which running plays?

Youth League

In *youth league* football, the coaches have to base the game plan on the strengths and weaknesses of their own players. The coach asks himself questions like: "Do my blockers control the line of scrimmage? Can my quarterback throw long passes with accuracy? Can my receivers catch long passes?" The answers to these questions help the coach decide what plays to use.

Giving the Game Plan to the Players

Once the coach decides on which plays will work best, he explains the plan to his players. He will probably show you diagrams of the plays and talk about how and when the plays will be run. Then you and your teammates will practice the plays. During the game, the quarterback must be able to call the plays quickly, and all players must understand the plays, or the strategy won't work.

In youth league football, the coach will give the plays to the quarterback during the game, either by sending a player to the huddle from the sidelines, or by signaling to the quarterback.

Plan the Plays, Play the Plan

Once your coach has *planned the plays*, it's the players' jobs to *play out the plan*. This means that you should have faith in your assignment and stick to it. Don't change your assignment in the middle of a play just because things aren't going well.

The coach will come up with two different game plans: one for the offensive team, and one for the defensive team.

Offensive Strategies

The plan for the offensive team will include plays that work well against the kind of defense that is usually used in your league. The coach will also pick plays that take advantage of his player's strengths and make up for their weaknesses.

If you have a big, strong running back who's quicker than most defenders, the coach will use a lot of running plays.

If you team's ball handlers can catch reliably, and can outrun most defensive backs, and if your quarterback can pass accurately, the coach will use a lot of pass plays.

If the guys on your team are smaller than the defenders, or if your guys aren't very fast, then the plan will be to out-think the other team by running a lot of fakes.

Your coach will probably use a variety of different plays so the defense won't be able to predict what you will do next.

Here's some plays that your offensive team might use:

Strategies for Running Plays

Basic running routes can be planned before the game. For example: the coach may plan to send the runners up the middle, or around the end, or have them run a fake, depending on what the runners do best. A small runner might get tackled trying to make it up the middle where there's a lot of linebackers. But if the small runner is also fast, then he can probably beat the defenders when he runs to the outside where there will be less traffic.

Only the first part of the routes can be planned out ahead of time, because once you are running your route, you will need to cut (change direction) to wherever there's an opening.

Sometimes the coach will decide on the routes during the game in order to take advantage of the formation the defenders are using. If the defense has a lot of players in the middle of the field, it's a good strategy to send your runners to the outside. If the defensive linebackers are playing on the outside of the defensive ends, leaving the middle open, then it makes sense to send your runners up the middle.

Strategies for Passing Plays

Your coach might use a *pass route tree* to assign the pass routs to the receivers. The pass route tree is a way of assigning numbers to the different pass routes. The number tells the receiver which route to run. On odd numbers the receiver will break to his left at a certain depth downfield. On even numbers, the receiver will break to his right at a certain depth downfield.

The quarterback will call out the pass patterns for all three receivers by saying three numbers in a row. For example, he might say, "eight, five, seven." This means that Receiver X's assignment is pass route eight, Receiver Y's is route five, and Receiver Z's is route seven. (X refers to the split end, Y refers to the tight end, and Z is the wide receiver.)

Whether your coach decides to use short passing patterns or long ones depends on several things:

- Short passes give the defenders fewer chances to intercept.

- Short passes are used if the quarterback has difficulty throwing long and accurately, or if his blockers are having trouble holding the line.

- Long passes are a good choice if: your quarterback can throw accurately at a distance, your blockers can give him time to pass, and you have a receiver who's fast and consistent.

Defensive Strategies

The job of the defense is to stop the offense from moving the ball toward their goal, and to try to get the ball back. Since the defense doesn't know the offense's plan (run or pass, stay short or go deep), the defenders have to be ready for anything. They have to "react" to what the offense does. Reacting means that they figure out what the offense will do, then act to stop them.

The game plan for the defense is mapped out before the game, but it can change, depending on what the other team is doing.

Stack Right and Stack Left

One way to confuse the offensive blockers and maybe cause them to mess up their assignments is for the defense to change their positions just before the ball is snapped. The coach signals either *stack right* or *stack left*. The defense lines up on the field in one alignment and just before the ball is snapped, the defensive linemen move either to the right or the left.

Strategies for Running Plays

Here are some defensive strategies that work well when the other team is running the ball:

Pinch

If your coach thinks the offense will run a play up the middle, he signals for a *pinch*, meaning that the guards and tackles will "shoot their gaps" (run between blockers), in order to stay in the middle of the field.

Slant Right

If the coach thinks the offense is going to run to the right side, then he signals *slant right*, and the tackles and the nose tackle will slant to the right and the outside linebacker on the right will cross the line of scrimmage and be ready to turn to the inside.

Slant Left

If the coach thinks that the offense is going to run up the left side of the field, then he signals *slant left*. The linemen and line- backers then move to the left.

Strategies for Passing Plays

Here are some strategies that are used when the other team is passing the ball:

Zone Coverage

In *zone coverage*, each defender will have an assigned area of the field to cover. That way, wherever the ball is thrown, there will be a defender in the area.

Man-to-Man Coverage

In *man-to-man coverage*, each defender has a certain offensive player to cover. That way, someone is certain to be covering the ball carrier or pass receiver.

The Blitz

On the *blitz*, up to eight defenders are assigned to rush the passer (go for the quarterback). The idea is that one of them will be able to get to the quarterback and sack him. Even if the defenders can't sack the quarterback, the blitz will force him to throw quickly to get rid of the ball before he gets tackled, and his throw probably won't be accurate.

Keep Focused

Make It Up, Play It Out

A game of fours gives defensive players lots of practice in reacting to what the offense is doing.

Fours

You need four or more players, a football, and a field. The offense tries to get as far downfield as possible in four downs. The offense has a quarterback and pass receivers. The defense has a timer and pass defenders. There is no running with the ball.

The timer counts four seconds out loud. The quarterback has to throw the ball before the count of four. When the offense completes a pass, it moves to that position on the field to start the next play. After four downs, teams switch sides. The team that gets the farthest down the field, gets a point for that round. The first team to get ten points is the winner.

If you are playing for the offense, remember to stay with your assignment, even if the play is breaking down.

If you're playing for the defense, you will want to stay with your assignment most of the time, but watch the offense to see what they are likely to be doing. If you can tackle the ball carrier, or protect your quarterback better by adjusting your move, then go ahead and make the change.

How did you get interested in football?
My dad was a coach so it became a part of our family life.

Did your dad influence your football career?
Yes, it was natural because he was coaching. and I always paid attention to what he was doing. I grew up on the football field, but I didn't play organized football until the seventh grade.

Did you always want to be a quarterback?
I guess so, but I didn't make it at first and I wound up playing tight end. Then the kid who beat me out moved away. If he hadn't moved, I'd probably still be playing tight end.

Is there a lesson for those who aren't successful the first time they play football?
Never give up. If you don't get to play the position you want, try another position. Or if the coach moves you to another position play it as hard as you can.

Do you get nervous before an NFL game?
I get nervous which makes me sleepy. I put on all my pads and go into the weight room where it's quiet and take a 15-minute nap to calm down.

How do you define a winner in sports?
It's someone who competes all the time and does everything possible to help the team win.

Glossary

Audible play changes—When the quarterback needs to change the play at the line of scrimmage, he uses a spoken code to tell his team about the change.

Backpedal—Running backward.

Ball carrier—The player who is carrying the ball while trying to move it toward the opponent's goal.

Blitz—When as many as eight defensive players rush the quarterback to try to sack him.

Block—Using your body to slow or stop an opponent.

Blocker—A player who uses his body to stop an opponent.

Bull block—A powerful block where the blocker explodes off the line of scrimmage and uses his forearms to move the defender to the outside and away from the quarterback.

Center—The player who lines up at the center of the offensive line on the line of scrimmage. The center puts the ball into play by snapping it through his legs to the quarterback.

Cover—A player covers an opponent by sticking with him and staying ready to stop him or keep him from catching a pass.

Cut block—A block used to cut off the defender before he can get to the quarterback.

Cutting—Changing direction very quickly.

Dead ball—When the ball is not in play. The ball is dead when it goes out of bounds and when the referee blows the whistle to end the play.

Defender—A defensive player.

Defense—The defense is the group of eleven players who defend your team's territory when the other team has the ball. When the other team has possession of the ball, then your defense is playing on the field.

Defensive backs—The backs line up behind the other defensive players. Their job is to tackle a ball carrier or pass receiver. Defensive backs are also known as cornerbacks and safeties.

Double team block—When two offensive linemen work together to block one defender.

Down—A play. A play lasts from the snap of the ball or the kick until the whistle is blown.

Drop kick—The player holds the ball in front of him, drops it, and kicks it.

End zone—The area at each end of the football field between the end line and the goal line. A touchdown is made when the football is run or passed into the other team's end zone.

Extra points—After a touchdown the scoring team can try for extra points. The ball is placed two yards from the goal line. If the ball is run or passed into the end zone, two extra points are earned. If the ball is kicked between the goal posts, one extra point is earned.

Fair catch—The receiver raises his arm above his head before catching a kicked ball. The signal means that he will not move once he has the ball, and that other players cannot tackle him.

Fake—Using body language to fool your opponent.

Field goal—When the ball is place-kicked through the goal posts for a score of three points.

Fifty-yard line—The yard line across the middle of the football field.

Fold block—A block made by two linemen where one lineman stops the defender and the other lineman crosses behind his teammate to finish the block.

Formation—The way the players are arranged on the field, waiting for the play to start.

Four-point stance—Taking a position where you have four points of contact with the ground —both feet and both hands.

Fumble—When the ball is dropped by a player before the end of the play.

Goal line—The "zero" yard line. A touchdown is made when the football is run or passed over the goal line.

Goal post—The goal post is shaped like a big H or Y with the crossbar of the goal post ten feet above the ground. There are two goal posts —one in each end zone. A field goal or extra point is made when the ball is kicked over the cross bar of the goal post.

Handoff—When the center gives the ball to the quarterback, or when the quarterback gives the ball to one of his teammates for a running play.

Huddle—When a team gets together on the field between plays to get their assignments from the quarterback.

I-formation—When two running backs are set up directly behind the quarterback.

Interception—When a defensive player catches a pass before the offensive receiver can catch it. The defensive player then gains possession of the ball for his team.

Jersey—The shirt worn by the players. The jersey is in the team's colors and has the player's number on the front and back.

Kicking play—A play where the ball is kicked.

Kickoff—A kick made from the forty-yard line of the kicking team that: starts the game, starts the second half of the game, or puts the ball back in play after a touchdown or field goal.

Linebackers—Defensive players that line up behind the defensive linemen at the line of scrimmage. The linebackers block and make tackles.

Line of scrimmage—An imaginary line that runs across the field where the ball is placed at the beginning of the play.

Linemen—There are offensive linemen and defensive linemen. They are the players who line up right on the line of scrimmage.

Man-to-man coverage—When each defensive player is assigned to cover a certain offensive player.

NCAA—National Collegiate Athletic Association.

NFL—National Football League

Nose tackle— When a defensive lineman sets up directly across the line of scrimmage from the center, he's called a nose tackle.

Offense—The offense is the group of eleven players who move the ball for your team. When your team has possession of the ball, then your offense is playing on the field.

Pass—When the ball is thrown from one player, usually the quarterback, to a teammate in order to move it toward the goal.

Passing play—A play where the ball is moved toward the goal by throwing it to a teammate.

Penalty—When a player breaks a rule, his team will be given a penalty by the referee. Penalties are usually loss of yardage.

Personal foul—Hitting an opponent with your fist, locked hands, forearm or elbow; kicking or kneeing another player; tripping, clipping or grasping another player's face mask; or tackling a player who does not have the ball are all personal fouls.

Place kick—The ball is held by a player or placed on a tee and kicked by that player's teammate.

Play action—A play where the quarterback fakes a handoff, then passes the ball.

Post pattern—A passing play where the receiver runs downfield and turns in the direction of the goal post.

Pro—A player who earns his living playing football. NFL players are pros.

Pro set—A formation in which two running backs set up five to seven yards behind the quarterback, with one running back out to the left of the quarterback, and the other running back out to the right of the quarterback..

Punt—A kick to send the ball down the field as far as possible before giving up the ball, usually on a fourth down.

Quarterback—The player who calls the plays for the offense. The quarterback also takes the snap from the center and either hands off or passes the ball to one of his teammates, who will try to more the ball toward the goal.

Receiver—A player who catches a pass, or a player who is allowed to catch a pass for his team.

Referee—An official who is on the field during the game to make sure the rules are obeyed. The referee signals the end of every play by blowing a whistle.

Running backs—Defensive players who block, take the ball from the quarterback and run it down the field, or catch passes and run to gain yardage. Running backs also fake the other team into thinking it's a running play when it's really a pass play.

Running play—a play where a runner carries the ball toward the goal line.

Sack—When the quarterback still has the ball and he is tackled behind the line of scrimmage.

Safety—When the offensive team loses yardage in a play and is pushed into their own end zone, and either loses the ball or is stopped by the other team. The other team scores two points.

Secondary—The secondary is made up of the defensive backs (cornerbacks and safeties).

Side line—There are two side lines, one on each side of the field. A player who crosses the sideline during a play is out of bounds.

Slant—A pass play where the receiver runs through the defense on an angle.

Snap—The play begins when the center gives or "snaps" the ball to the quarterback.

Special teams—In addition to the offense and defense, a football team has other, special teams that are used for kickoffs and punt returns.

Strategy—A plan of action. The game plan.

Streak pattern—A passing play where the receiver runs straight down the field.

Stripping—When a defender forces the ball carrier to drop the ball by grabbing his arms or knocking the ball out of his hands.

Tackle—The use of hands, arms, and body to stop the ball carrier. A player who tackles is also known as a tackle.

Territory—Each team has a territory, which is the half of the field that they are defending.

Three-point stance—Taking a position where you have three points of contact with the ground, your two feet and one hand.

Touchdown—When the ball is run or passed into the end zone for a score of six points.

Two-point stance—Taking a position where you have two points of contact with the ground —your two feet.

Zone coverage—When the defensive players are assigned to cover a certain area of the field.

Index

Adjusting on the move, 45
Angle, tackling on, 61–62

Backpedaling, 19, 69, 70
Backs:
    cornerbacks, 68–69
    defensive, 59, 68–71
Blake, Jeff, 28–29
Bledsoe, Drew, 86–87
Blitz, 4, 19, 39, 85
Blocking, 37–39
    bull, 38
    cut block, 38, 48
    double team block, 56, 57
    drive block, 56, 57
    fold block, 57
    kick-out, 37
    loco or straight ahead, 38
    pass block, 57
    stalk block, 48
    trap block, 58
Body language, 45

Catch the black dot, drill, 46
Catching the ball, 46–47
    fair catch, 79–80
Catching the pitch out, 34, 35
Center, 5, 55
    place-kicking, 74
    snapping the ball, 55
Charges, 63–65
    loop, 64–65
    shoot-the-gap, 65
    slant, 64, 65
Coach, 7, 81
Collins, Kerry, 50–51
Comeback patterns, 25, 44
Cornerbacks, 4, 68–69
Crossing patterns, 25, 44
Cut block, 48

Defender, pressure on, 44
Defense, 59–72
    basic formations, 60
    job of, 3, 59
    man-to-man, 68
    playing the game, 4
    receiver's moves in, 48
    strategies, 84–85
    tackling, 60–61
    zone, 68
Defensive linemen, 61–68
    charges or stunts, 63–65

setting up, 62–63
Double team block, 56, 57
Downs, 5
Draw play, 18
Drills:
    backpedal, 70
    catch the black dot, 46
    kicking, 75
    on the knee, throwing, 24
    lock on, 48
    push-pull, 58
    shed, 65
    stance and start, 34
    stumble, 36
    throw on the run, 26

Ends, 4, 5
Equipment, 3
Exercises, getting in shape, 7–9
Extra points, 6
Eye contact, 45
Eyes, and catching the ball, 46

Fair catch, 79–80
Faking, 37, 45
Field goals, 6
First down, 35
Flanker, job of, 5
Focus:
    blocking, 58
    defense, 72
    game plan, 85
    kicking, 80
    receivers, 49
    running backs, 40
    throwing the ball, 27
Football, 1–10
    ball, 2
    equipment, 3
    getting in shape for, 7–9
    getting started, 2–3
    players, 3
    playing the game, 4–6
    rules of, 6–7
Four-man line, four-three, 60
Four-point stance, 63
Fours, 85
Fullback, in offensive play, 5
Fumbling, 34

Game plan, 81–85
    defensive strategies, 84–85
    making, 81–82

offensive strategies, 82–83
Games:
    fours, 85
    kick return, 80
    pass pattern, 40
    quarterback toss, 27
    roll ball, 27
    shuttle, 49
    target rush, 71–72
    touch football, 10
Glossary, 89–90
Goal posts, 2
Grip, for throwing, 22
Guards, 53–55
    in offensive play, 5
    stance, 54
    take off, 54

Halfback, in offensive play, 5
Handoffs, 16–18, 34
    faking, 18
    front out, 16
    reverse pivot, 17
    toss, 17, 18
    underneath, 16
Hands:
    in catching the ball, 46
    of offensive linemen, 52
Hitch passes, 25, 44
Holder, place-kicking, 74–75
Hook passes, 25

I-formation, 33

Kicking drill, 75
Kicking game, 6, 73–80
    kick return team, 79–80
    place-kicking, 74–76
    punting, 77, 78
Kicking team, 73–78
Kickoff, 4, 74
    returning, 80

Lead player, 57
Leaving the ball untouched, 80
Linebackers, 67–68
    defensive, 4, 59
    setting up, 67
Linemen:
    defensive, 59, 61–68
    offensive, 53–58
Lock on drill, 48

Making cuts, 36
Man-to-man defense, 68, 70–71, 85
Moving the ball, 5–6

Nose tackle, 62

Offense, job of, 3, 5
Offensive linemen, 53–58
    center, 55
    guards and tackles, 53–55
    types of blocks, 56–58
Offensive strategies, 82–83
Officials, 7
Open area, finding, 46
Open field, tackling in, 61
Outs, in pass patterns, 44

Pass rush, 66
Pass drops, 20–22
Passes:
    types of, 25–26
    uncatchable, 46
Passing, 19–26
    on the numbers, 46
    separation in, 46
Passing plays, 6, 83, 84–85
Pass patterns:
    calling out, 83
    game, 40
    receivers, 44
    running backs, 39–40
    running moves for, 44–46
Pass route tree, 83
Pattern:
    from behind line of
        scrimmage, 39
    body language in, 45
    close-in, 39
    comeback, 44
    crossing, 44
    deep, 39
    outs, 44
    pass, 39, 40
    post, 44
    running, 39
    slant, 44
    streak, 44
Pinch, 84
Place-kicking, 74–76
Play action, 18
Playing field, 2
Pocket, 34
Points, extra, 6
Post pattern, 25, 44

Post player, 56
Pressure, on defender, 44
Pro set, 32, 33
Punt, returning, 79
Punting, 77, 78
Push-pull drill, 58

Quarterback, 5, 11–27
    calling the play, 11–12
    calling signals, 14–15
    changing the play, 12–13
    checking the defense, 12
    handoff, 16–18
    sacking, 65–67
    securing the ball, 15
    snap, 15
    snap count, 13
    starting the play, 13–18
Quarterback toss game, 27
Quick screen, 26
Quick square-out pass, 25, 44

Read screen, 26
Receivers, 41–49
    blocking, 48
    body language, 45
    body position, 47
    catching the ball, 46–47
    checking pass coverage, 43
    defensive moves, 48
    getting ready to run, 42–43
    pass patterns, 44–46
    tucking and running, 47
Referees, 7
Rip, 67
Roll ball game, 27
Running backs, 31–40
    blocking, 37–39
    faking, 37
    getting the ball, 32–35
    passing game, 39
    rules for, 39
    running with the ball, 35–37
Running plays, 5, 83, 84

Sacking the quarterback, 65–67
Safeties, 4, 6, 69
Scoring, 6
Scrimmage, line of, 4
Secondary backs, 68
Semi-sprint pass, 22
Separation, 46
Shed drill, 65
Shuttle game, 49

Slant pass, 25, 44
Slant right, slant left, 84
Snap, 15, 55
Snap count, 13
Special teams, 3
Sprint-out pass, 20
Stack right and stack left, 84
Stalk block, 48
Stance:
    center, 55
    defensive backs, 70
    four-point, 63
    goal line and short yardage, 64
    guards and tackles, 54
    linebacker, 68
    quarterback, 13–14
    three-point, 62, 63
Stance and start drill, 34
Streak pattern, 26, 44
Stripping, 37, 70–71
Stumble drill, 36
Stunt charges, 63–65
Swim, 67
Swing and screen passes, 26

Tackles, 5, 53–55
    stance, 54
    take off, 54
Tackling, 60–61
    sacking the quarterback, 65–67
Target rush game, 71–72
Territories, 2
Three-man line, three-four, 60
Three-point stance, 62, 63
Throwing the ball, 22–24
Throw on the run, drill, 26
Timing, 4
Touchdowns, 6
Touch football, 10
Tucking and running, 47

Zone defense, 68, 70–71, 85